RECENT ADVANCES IN STEGANOGRAPHY

Edited by **Hedieh Sajedi**

Recent Advances in Steganography
http://dx.doi.org/10.5772/2501
Edited by Hedieh Sajedi

Contributors
Farid Ghareh Mohammadi, Mohammad Saniee Abadeh, Blanca E. Carvajal-Gámez, Francisco J. Gallegos-Funes, Alberto J. Rosales-Silva, Rene Santiago-Cruz, Hedieh Sajedi, Yildiray Yalman, Feyzi Akar, Ismail Erturk, Naofumi Aoki

Published by InTech
Janeza Trdine 9, 51000 Rijeka, Croatia

Publishing Process Manager Oliver Kurelic
Typesetting InTech Prepress, Novi Sad
Cover InTech Design Team

First published October, 2012
Printed in Croatia

A free online edition of this book is available at www.intechopen.com
Additional hard copies can be obtained from orders@intechopen.com

Recent Advances in Steganography, Edited by Hedieh Sajedi
p. cm.
ISBN 978-953-51-0840-5

Meet the editor

Dr. Hedieh Sajedi received a B.Sc. degree in Computer Engineering from AmirKabir University of Technology in 2003, and M.Sc. and Ph.D degrees in Computer Engineering (Artificial Intelligence) from Sharif University of Technology, Tehran, Iran in 2006 and 2010, respectively. She is currently an Assistant Professor at the Department of Computer Science, Tehran University, Iran. She has presented several papers about steganography and steganalysis in well-known Journals and Conferences. Her research interests include Multimedia data hiding, steganography and steganalysis methods, pattern recognition, and machine learning.

Contents

Preface

The information concealment concerns the process of integrating information or data elements into images, video, and music. This book presents the latest advances in the area of Steganography, a relatively new technique in information hiding.

In chapter 1, steganalysis is introduced as the task of discovering the presence of secret data. Data mining is the research area involving powerful processes and tools that allow an effective analysis and exploration of data. In particular, data mining techniques have found application in numerous different scientific fields, with the aim of discovering previously unknown patterns and correlations, as well as predicting trends and behaviors. The first chapter provides an overview of the various data mining techniques used for steganalysis.

Chapter 2 by Carvajal-Gamez,et al. introduces steganography in different colour models using an energy adjustment applying Wavelets. In this chapter, a scaling factor depending directly on the number of bits of the host image is proposed to ensure that the use of steganographic technique does not affect the host image and the hidden information is not visible to the HVS. Applying the scaling factor the energy generated by the host image is preserved to approximate the original image, eliminating any visual disturbance, being imperceptible to the human eye.

Chapter 3 introduces rule-based adaptive batch steganography. In batch steganography the secret data is hidden in more than one image. In the approach presented is this chapter, the secret data is split and embedded based on the features of the cover images. Experimental verification demonstrates the utility of the approach in hiding large secret data.

Chapter 4 by Yalman et al. investigates contemporary approaches to the histogram modification based on data hiding techniques. The stego images that are produced by using such data hiding techniques are inherently robust against main geometrical attacks such as rotation, scattered tiles and warping, as well as other main attacks. An up-to-date method and its example application to the latest histogram modification based steganography methods and its results are presented in detail and compared to those of the classical ones.

Chapter 5 by Aoki describes lossless steganography for speech communications. There is no way to avoid inevitable degradation of speech data by embedding secret message with the LSB replacement technique. In order to mitigate this problem, this chapter describes an idea of the lossless steganography technique for telephony communications. The proposed technique exploits the characteristic of the folded binary code employed in several speech codecs, such as G.711 and DVI-ADPCM.

The presented book will be valuable to both academia and industry. Researchers in the departments of electrical/electronics/communication engineering, computer science and relating departments will find this book useful.

We appreciate the authors of the chapters for their interest in contributing. We hope that the readers will benefit from this book.

Hedieh Sajedi
Department of Computer Science,
Tehran University,
Iran

1

A Survey of Data Mining Techniques for Steganalysis

Farid Ghareh Mohammadi and Mohammad Saniee Abadeh
Faculty of Electrical and Computer Engineering, Tarbiat Modares University
Iran

1. Introduction

The skill of observing the invisible embedded messages in images, audio, video, text as multimedia and protocols called Steganalysis. An efficient steganalysis method should determine the existence of implanted messages and stego digital image and present some results about the used steganographic algorithm. The challenging problem of this study is a massive quantity of stego hosts to learn valuable knowledge. In this paper, we propose to study several current data mining approaches on steganalysis of images, audio, video, text and protocol. The main aim of this survey is to present the efficiency of using data mining techniques in steganalysis in comparison to the model based steganalysis approaches.

The skill and knowledge of identifying secret message concealed by steganography approach is called Steganalysis. Steganalysis is the skill of detecting the existence of the concealed data in digital images, texts, audios, videos, protocols (Nissar & Mir, 2010). Steganalysis can be categorized into two groups: (a) static and (b) dynamic. Guesstimate some parameter(s) of the embedded algorithm or the secret message is the target of dynamic steganalysis, identifies the existence/non-existence of a secret message is the aim of static steganalysis; in other word these two groups have additional definitions as below:

Static steganalysis: discovering the existence/non-existence of a concealed message in a stego file and recognizing the stego embedded algorithm.

Dynamic steganalysis: guesstimating the implanted message length, position(s) of the concealed message, the secret key used in implanting, some parameters of the stego implanting algorithm and take out the concealed message.

An operation that takes out a number of novel nontrivial patterns included in huge records or databases is called Data Mining. Data Mining includes the utilization of complicated data analysis, which means to find out earlier unidentified, forensic patterns and associations in myriad data set. Therefore, data mining involves analysis, forecast, gathering and organizing data. The aim of data mining is to realize hidden models, unforeseen styles or data, exploiting a mixture of methods from machine learning to bio-inspired meta-heuristic algorithms. Multiple main phases of data mining operation consist of (1) Scope perceptive; (2) Data choice; (3) Data pre-processing, clear out and training; (4) Realizing patterns; (5) Explanation; and (6) Exposure and utilizing revealed facts (Bhatt & Kankanhalli, 2011).

In this study, we will present the survey of using data mining techniques on steganalysis, with intention to establish the significant data mining methods such as classification, clustering and other data mining methods that have been applied for steganalysis purposes. We will review numerous classification methods containing Decision Tree (DT), Support Vector Machines (SVM), Naive Bayes (NB), K-nearest neighbour (KNN), Neural Network (NN) and also a major variety of clustering methods contain K-means, agglomeration and random algorithms.

The rest of this book chapter is organized as follows: In Section 2, we will review the general classification of data mining techniques on steganalysis. Section 3 discusses about applied data mining techniques in brief. In Section 4, we will discuss the applied data mining techniques for image steganalysis. We will study data mining techniques for steganalysis over audio, video, text and protocol domains in section 5. In section 6, we will summarize several previous investigations about the application of data mining techniques for steganalysis using several well-presented figures and tables. Section 7 concludes this book chapter.

2. General categorization of data mining techniques on steganalysis

The aim of this section is to present an immediate wide spread picture of the importance of mixing data mining techniques. By using data mining algorithms we detect secret and hidden concealed message through steganalysis. We have several kinds of data types assigned as Domain that should be considered such as: Image, Audio, Text, Video and Protocol. This classification is based on data mining techniques extended on steganalysis in this domain which are used to detect the presence of embedded messages in stego images by steganography techniques. Under each of them, the domains are further sub-divided into data mining techniques. The whole hierarchy of the categorization is shown in fig 1.

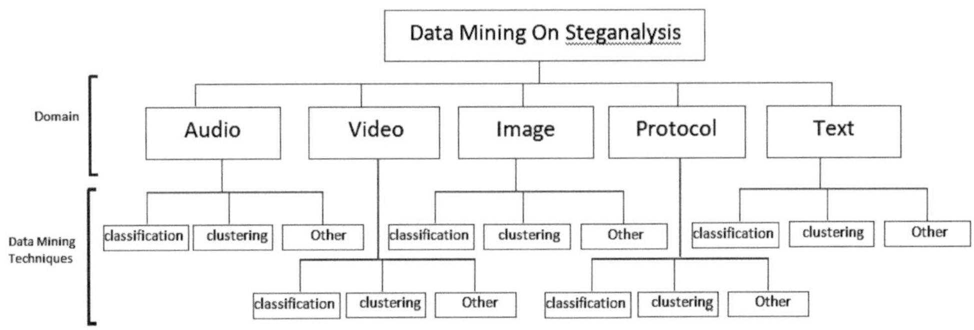

Fig. 1. The hierarchy of the General Categorization of Data Mining techniques on steganalysis.

These sub-domains (data mining techniques) are sub-divided into approaches which are applied in:

- Classification, which has been divided into neural network (NN), k-nearest neighbour (KNN), Support Vector Machine (SVM), Decision Tree (DT), Naive Bayes (NB) approaches. This category has itself a hierarchy which is shown in Fig. 2.

- Clustering, which has been divided into K-means, agglomeration and random algorithms.
- Other data mining tasks, such as regression approaches and etc.

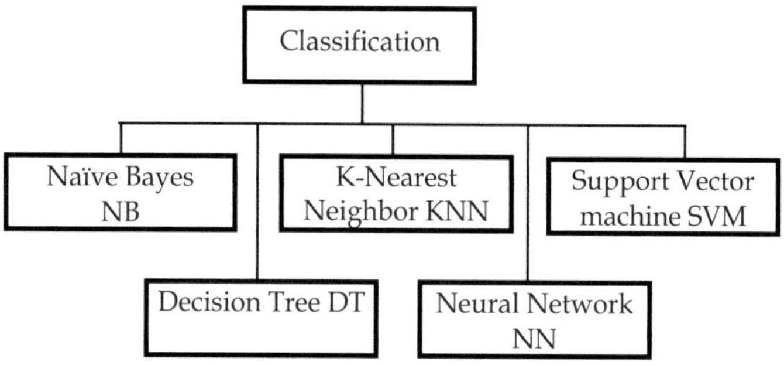

Fig. 2. The hierarchy of the category classification approach.

3. Overview of data mining techniques

As we aim to provide the general data mining techniques on steganalysis scheme, some definitions of applied techniques, need to be introduced:

Naive Bayes Classification (NB): A Naive Bayes classifier is a simple probabilistic classifier based on applying Bayes' theorem with strong independence assumptions. A more descriptive term for the underlying probability model would be an independent feature model. (Kaipa & Robila, 2010).

Decision Tree classification (DT): A Decision Tree, more properly a classification tree, is mostly used to learn a classification model which predicts the value of a dependent attribute (variable) given the values of the independent (input) attributes (variables). This solves a problem known as supervised classification since the dependent attribute and the number of classes (values) that it may have are given. (Kaipa&Robila, 2010). In decision tree structures, leaves signify classifications and branches signify a combination of characteristics that direct to those classifications (Duda et al, 2001).

Support Vector Machine (SVM) Classification: The aim of SVMs is to learn a model which forecasts class tag of cases in the testing set. This classification algorithm is one of the most robust classifiers for two-class classification. SVM can manage both linear and nonlinear classification problems. For linear discrete problems, SVM classifiers purely explore for a hyper-plane that distinguishes negative and positive instances (Cortes & Vapnik, 1995), (Vapnik, 1998), (Boser et al, 1992).

In the terminology of SVM literature, an attribute is a forecaster variable and a feature is an attribute which is applied to describe the hyper-plane. Feature selection is the operation of selecting the most appropriate attribute. SVM method is strongly correlated to neural networks. In fact, Support Vector Machine (SVM) methods have a close relation to traditional N-layer perceptron neural networks (Hernandez et al, 2008).

K-Nearest Neighbour classification (KNN): One kind of supervised classification techniques is called K-nearest neighbour classifier. KNN presented by Devijver and Kittler (Devijver &

Kittler, 1982), commonly use the Euclidean distance measure. For each row of the test set, the k nearest (in Euclidean distance) training set vectors are found, and the classification is decided by majority vote, with ties broken at random. If there are ties for the kth nearest vector, all candidates are included in the vote.

Neural Network classification (NN): One kind of classification techniques is called a neural network classifier. The important problem in a neural network is that convergence is not fast. Practically, this is the most important restriction of neural network applications, because data hiding method is not a linear method, if we only employ linear classification technique to categorize images. The neural network has an admirable facility to simulate any nonlinear correlation. Therefore, it has been used to categorize images. Neural network draws on three levels: input level, hidden level and output level (Liu et al, 2003).

Agglomerative Clustering: Agglomerative hierarchical clustering is a bottom-up clustering approach where clusters have sub-clusters, which in turn have sub-clusters, etc. The classic example of this is species taxonomy. Gene expression data might also demonstrate this hierarchical quality (e.g. Neurotransmitter gene families). Agglomerative hierarchical clustering begins with every single object (gene or sample) in a single cluster. This algorithm merges the closest pair of clusters in each iteration. This merging is accomplished by satisfying some similarity criteria, until all of the data are in a single cluster (Ker & Pevny, 2011).

4. Data mining techniques on steganalysis over the image

In this section we present data mining techniques in image domain that divided into three parts. In the first part, we introduce classification approaches in image steganalysis such as: support vector machine (SVM), k nearest neighbour (KNN), neural network (NN), naive Bayes (NB) and decision tree (DT). In the second part, we present clustering approaches in image steganalysis such as: K-means, random clustering, agglomerative and other data mining methods such as: Regression.

4.1 Classification techniques used on steganalysis

4.1.1 Support Vector Machine Classification (SVM)

Support vector machines (SVMs) have been broadly used as a categorizer device with an enormous deal of achievement from steganalysis to categorization of the presents of stego grams. The SVMs present supervised ML (machine learning) methods to generate a model which forecasts the goal values of the examination data specified only the experiment data attributes and discover the most favourable discrete hyper spheres which split the test data into two or N-groups for classification. A four-process sampling technique used to take out the image facial appearance (characteristic) for steganalysis. Applying a two-class SVM classifier, Lou and his colleagues are capable to make distinction cover images from the stego-images with an accuracy of 98.51%. Applying N-class SVM classifier, an estimator which is capable of detecting the secret key with an accuracy of 99.77% is created. See (Lou et al., 2011) for an example of SVM as the steganalysis technique.

A well-organized universal steganalysis plan is suggested by Lou and his colleagues to distinguish clear images from stego images in frequency and spatial domains (Lou et al,

2009). The suggested plan is executed in four phases: feature databases set, features mining, categorized from learning and length calculating approximately. The feature of databases would be explained in the first phase and the numerical features of the learning sets would be taken out in the following phase. After that, a number of two-class SVM based models would be learned by the mined features and the length of distrustful images would be recognized by the evaluation strategy in the final phase. The aim of SVMs was to discover the most favourable discriminate hyper sphere which shares the mined features into two collections in the utmost scope.

In (Joo et al, 2010), Joo and his colleagues suggest a steganalysis plan to disclose the presence of the concealed message like as the encoded data. The goal of this paper is to demonstrate that a distrustful image was customized by information concealing methods. Because the actual image has a high correlation amongst the adjacent pixels, the message put into modifies the pixel value and the diversity among the pixels. Thus, it builds the chunk effect and the correlation with the neighbouring pixels is broken. So, the diversity histogram of the 1- line cropped altered-image is different to that of the primary changed-image. Blind features suggested are the space measures among the diversity histogram of the main and the cut image. The presentation of the suggested steganalysis is verified throughout a huge and different image set. The Support Vector Machine (SVM) has used two categories that are normal and changed images. To identify that a distrustful image consists of an unseen message or not, the LIBSVM was used (Chang & Lin, 2001) as a strong two-class categorizer. All the images were equally shared non-overlap testing and learning subsets. The SVM categorizer was trained by the characteristic values of 1000 normal and 4000 changed-images.

In (Hernandez et al, 2008), numerical moment of wavelet feature function and neural network (NN) method is offered for a progress to the steganalysis as a classifier. Preceding research have declared that this steganalysis scheme has an excellent performance in the discovery of stego-image produced by diverse steganography techniques, but it has troubles to the steganography depend on bit plane complex segmentation (BPCS), this steganalysis has illustrated a little discovery speed of stego-image, produced by BPCS steganography, as a result, suggested effort offered to apply a support vector machine (SVM) as classifier instead of ANN. As a result, when SVM is applied instead to ANN investigation results descriptive significantly enhance of BPCS recognition rate (at least 20%).

In (Sajedi & Jamzad, 2008), the authors proposed a novel universal method for steganalysis, which utilizes numerical moments of contourlet coefficients as characteristics for examination. An SVM based non-linear classifier is applied to categorize stego and cover images. The efficiency of the suggested technique is determined by extensive tentative analysis. The suggested steganalysis technique is compared with two steganalyzers and versus usual steganography techniques. The results declared the prior performance of suggested technique.

In (Marvel et al, 2008), Marvel and his colleagues suggested blend N-rate-specific. The rate-specific categorizers SVM parameter (e.g., Far from every model over-plane) is utilized as entrance to the blending categorizer. Marvel and his colleagues determined the act of this practice and compare it with the universal categorizer and the rate-specific categorizer.

In (Mehrabiet al, 2007), the authors proposed a novel image steganalysis system which was depended on numerical moments of the histogram of N-level wavelet sub bands in frequency scope. Different frequencies of histogram have different sensitivity to various data embedding. The first three statistical moments of each band are selected to form a 78-dimensional feature vector for steganalysis. An SVM based classifier is then used to discriminate between stego and clear images.

In (Zou et al, 2006), the authors have suggested steganalysis scheme which depends on a 2-D Markov chain thresholded forecast-error image. Image pixels are forecasted with their adjacenting pixels, and the forecast-error image is produced by decreasing the calculated value of the pixel value and then thresholded with a predefined threshold. The practical conversion matrixes of Markov chains beside the vertical, horizontal, and crosswise instructions assist as structures for steganalysis. For feature ordering, the SVM with whether linear cores and also non-linear cores are utilized as categorizer. The non-linear as one of SVM methods executes considerably more superior than the linear SVM for their suggested structures. The trial outcomes have verified that the recommended steganalysis characteristics are more operative than that offered in (Sullivan et al, 2005) for proposed spread spectrum steganography techniques and more operative than the wavelet-base structures suggested in (Lyu et al, 2002) for LSB steganography methods.

Chen and his colleagues presented a novel universal steganalysis technique depends on numerical moments consequent from either JPEG 2-Dand an image 2-Darray. Furthermore, the head direction histogram, the second direction histogram is measured. The support vector machine (SVM) is applied in (Chen et al, 2006) as a classifier. The SVM used (Chen et al, 2006) as classifier instead of NN techniques with regard to its comparable act and more effective computation.

In (Liu & Sung, 2007), Liu & Sung presented a structure of steganalysis for LSB based steganography algorithms in blend black and white images. Their method depended on feature extracting and Neuro-fuzzy deduction schemes. Four kinds of features mined, based on DENFIS feature choice applied, and SVM-RFE applied to get better detection accuracy.

4.1.2 Naive Base and Decision Tree Classification (NB & DT)

In (Kaipa & Robila, 2010), suggested to plan and operate a scheme capable of categorizing the images into clear and stego images by typical shape classification methods like as Naive Bayes (NB) and Decision Trees (DT). Experiments have shown on a huge file set of images to specify the classification technique that executes the best comparing classification fault and achievement degrees in every item. Kaipa and Robila have used Weka, a software program application on data mining scope advanced in Java for suggested destination. Kaipa and Robila have also advanced a program by Weka Java library aimed at filling the files of the Images and categorize the images into clear images and stego-images.

In (Liu et al., 2006), the authors presented various numerical design detection techniques which are used to train and categorize the characteristic sets. Comparison of suggested technique and another, shows suggested technique is extremely efficient. It is vastly effectual for color image steganalysis. It is also fit for black and white color steganalysis in the little image density and intricacy scope.

In (Benton & Chu, 2005), the authors presented using decision trees (DT) and neural networks (NN) to categorize the images into stego and clear images. Ryan and Henry investigated by applying decision trees (DT) for discovering message concealed in the LSBP of an image and compare their outcomes to those achievements applying N-layered feed frontward NN.

In (Berg et al., 2003), Berg and his colleagues showed the possibility of utilizing a data mining and machine learning (DM/ML) method to robotically construct as steganalysis methods. For either compression-based (JPEG) or content-based (GIF) an image form, DM/ML methods are so magnificently capable to separate clean files from stego-ones. The suggested method is depending on an image figure of the media form that builds obvious completion of the structures that can be applied for steganographic implanting. They have revealed how this could be blended with a group of features chosen for the picture depicts. In suggested effort, that contains value happening chances, and either conditional or unconditional entropies. These structures were positively applied, for each JEPG and GIF types, and by the use a number of diverse training processes, to discovery concealed message carrying out files. They find out that the three training methods attempted consist of artificial neural network (ANN), decision trees (DT) and naive Bayes (NB) classifiers accomplished suggestively more improved than arbitrary estimating in a diversity of conditions.

4.1.3 K-Nearest Neighbour Classification (KNN)

Presented an approach for steganalysis scheme depends on a group of 193 features with two major aims: first, demonstrates adequate amount of images of operative training of a categorizer in they got upper-dimensional space, and second, utilizes feature selection to select greatest related structures for the favoured categorization. Dimensionality reduction is achieved applying a frontward selection and decreases the primary 193 feature fixed by element of 13, using totally similar performance. In (Miche et al, 2007) two diverse kinds of categorizers have mostly been applied: the first one, K-nearest neighbours (KNN), for its totally efficient presentation even in upper dimensional space, but totally, since it is very speedy. SVM approach was similarly selected because it is amongst the classifiers presented the greatest outcomes. The main disadvantage is of process the calculating time.

In (Miche et al, 2006), the authors presented an approach to choice structures earlier learning and test a classifier depend on Support Vector Machines (SVM) approach. In suggested work 23 features provided by Fridrich were evaluated. K-Nearest-Neighbours (KNN) is a feature grading that is achieved applying a quick classifier mixed with a forward selection. The product of the feature selection is subsequently verified on support vector machine (SVM) to choose the optimum amount of features. Suggested technique is tried by the Outguess steganographic approach and 14 features are chosen while supporting the equal classification performances. Outcomes approve that the chosen features are well-organized for an extensive variety of implanting rates. The similar approach is used for F5 and Steghide method to conceive if feature selection is capable on suggested process.

4.1.4 Neural Network Classification (NN)

In (Shaohui et al, 2003), the authors presented a novel technique based on neural network (NN) to get numerical features of images to detect the essential concealed data. Shaohui and his colleagues discovered that neural network (NN) approach cannot be applied to linear problems and is more practical to nonlinear problems, so in their suggested paper Shaohui and his colleagues utilize BP neural network (NN) to simulate and train images. Suggested BP neural network (NN) applied a three layer NN consists of an input layer, hidden layer and output layer. This technique discovers statistically indicates after original images has been concealed message, then utilizing the ability of estimation of neural network (NN)for demonstrating either an image is non-stego or stego image.

A blind image steganalysis scheme is proposed, in which feature is consists of the numerical moments of characteristic functions of the test image, the prediction-error image and their wavelet sub bands. The approach of categorizer is another main factor in steganalysis. In (Shi et al, 2005), the feed forward NN with BP learning process is utilized as the categorizer. It is the strong training ability influenced by using the NN will overtake the linear categorizers. In the examining step, the non-linear NN outputs offers lower classification rate than the linear outputs.

In (Liul et al, 2004), the authors presented actual features through means of quality analysis from clear images and stego images, after that, applying neural network(NN) approach as a separator to differentiate non-stego-images and stego-images. Liul and his colleagues utilized BP neural network (NN) to approve their approach. The first phase is to learn and test neural network (NN) to acquire network parameters. In spite these parameters, they could simulate the outcomes. This BP neural network (NN) applies three layers: input one, hidden one and output one. In neural network (NN), they adjust a number of characteristics as the certain nerve cells of the input layer.

In (kobsi & merouani, 2007), the authors presented methods depend on Neural Network (NN) that are acceptable to distinguish its efficiency for steganalysis.

In (Holoska et al., 2010), the authors suggested a blind steganalysis method which depends on a universal neural network (NN) approach and matches it to Stegdetect - a kind of tool that uses a linear classification device.

In (Sabeti et al, 2010), the authors presented Five different N-level perceptron neural network (NN) approaches trained to discover diverse layers of implanting. Every image is served to all systems and electing scheme classifies the image as either cover images or stego images. The operation outcomes show 88.6% achieved in the true classification of the test images that involved in at least 20% embedding rate and the rest 14% success in the true classification of the test images involved at most 20% imbedding rate. Every system in the categorizer was independently trained with feature groups mined from 150 stego-images and 150 cover images embedded with the used fraction of capacity. Every test image was applied once as clear and about five times, through diverse layers of implanting, as a stego image.

4.2 Clustering and other data mining techniques applied over the images

In (Ker &Pevny, 2011), the authors suggested a technique which depends on clustering more preferably than classification. This new presented method efficiently evaluates the performance of performers by supposing that the greatest of them are cleared: after applying the agglomerative hierarchical clustering method, the guilty performer(s) is clustered distinct from the non-guilty majority. Suggested paper training indicates that is used in the instance of JPEG images.

In (Tuia et al, 2010), the authors presented non-passive sampling to tag pixels set with hierarchical clustering. The goal of suggested technique is to compare the data relations exposed by the clustering process. Explorations the trimming of the hierarchy diagram as a tree is performed by an active learning process which best matches the tags of the sampled cases. By selecting the portion of the tree to model according to trimming's indecision, instance selecting is concentrated in utmost indecision clusters.

In (Rodriguez et al, 2007), the authors presented a study of the method and essential attentions integral in the expansion of a novel technique used for the discovery of concealed files into digital images. Rodriguez and his colleagues determined the efficiency of one of clustering methods called Learning Vector Quantization (LVQ) that supports in discriminating clean images from abnormal or non-clear images. This comparison is treated applying 7 features (Agaian et al, 2006) over a less group of 200 explanations with different layers of embedded data from 1% up 10% in increases of 1%. The outcomes determined that LVQ as clustering method not only, more perfectly detect when an image includes LSB concealed data when matched to another clustering method such as: k-means or utilizing the primary feature sets, but also gives a simple technique for demonstrating the fraction of imbedding given non-high data imbedding fractions.

In (Avcıbas et al, 2003), the authors presented methods for steganalysis of images that both the active and passive warden frameworks have been possibly exposed to steganographic processes. Then proposed a categorizer between stego images and non-stego-images which are made applying multivariate regression method on the designated quality metrics and is trained depends on an appraisal of the primary image. Simulation outcomes with the selected feature group and recognized steganographic methods show that suggested method is capable with realistic truthfulness to discriminate between stego-images and non-stego images.

In (Cho et al, 2010), the authors aimed to plan one n-classifier that categorizes non-clear images based on their steganographic processes in order to distinctive cover images from stego-images. This organization is depending on steganalysis outcomes of disintegrated image chunks. As an actual image frequently contains non-homogeneous areas, its disintegration will toward lesser image chunks, each of that is more non-heterogeneous. Cho and his colleagues classified those image chunks into N-classes and discover a categorizer for per class to decide either a chunk is from a non-stego image or a stego image with a certain steganographic process.

In (Lin et al, 2004), the authors proposed a technique of identifying the presence of embedded messages, that are arbitrarily spread in the least significant hits (LSB) of 1byteblack and white images and 3byte RGB colour images. The proposed discover scheme depends on the one of data mining techniques like support vector regression (SVR) technique. It is revealed that the quantity of a designated group of characteristic models a n-dimensional feature space that permits approximation of the size of concealed messages imbedded in the LSB of non-stego images with most accuracy.

5. Data mining techniques on steganalysis over multimedia and protocol

In this section we present several data mining techniques used to steganalysis over Audio, Text, Video and Protocol domains. The percentage of papers referenced to data mining approaches over these domains are about 20% and its lesser than image, for this reason we separate our work into two parts, which in the previous part we proposed data mining techniques on steganalysis over Image that contains 80% of all paper that used and referenced, and in this part, we survey data mining approaches over Audio, Text, Video and Protocol domains.

5.1 Data mining techniques on steganalysis over Audio

In (Geetha et al, 2010), the authors present a useful forensic steganalysis method for audio signals which can appropriately evaluate the measurements troubled by non-clear imbedding and categorize them to designate recent steganographic approaches. A summary of a rule based approach with six kinds of decision tree categorizer like as: Decision Stump, Naive Bayes, Alternating Decision Tree, Fast Decision Tree, J48 Tree and Logical Model Tree initiate, presented to achieve the discovery of the audio subliminal network. The assessment of the decision tree model and the boosted feature space, on a dataset include 4800 non stego and stego audio archives are accomplished for the traditional stenographic approach.

In (Kraetzer et al, 2007), the authors presented a method for digital media forensics to demonstrate the utilized microphones and the situations around of recorded digital audio examples of utilizing recognized audio steganalysis characteristic. Suggested main assessment is depended on a restricted prototypical test group of 10 diverse kinds of audio reference signals listed as single audio records using four microphones in 10 diverse places with 2byte digitalization and 44.1 kHz arbitrary model ratio. Suggested opinion was primarily determined through the presence steganalysis features and the request of usages in a restricted test and the first set. In the suggested tests, an inter-tool inquiry and evaluation with diverse tool features is achieved while intra-tool assessments are unconsidered. One kind of the data mining tools is WEKA that used for categorization consists of K-means approach as a kind of the clustering method and Naive Bayes (NB) approach as a kind of classification method are used with the aim to assess their categorization in respect to the categorization correctness on recognizing audio steganalysis features.

In (Ruetal, 2005), the author presented a steganalysis technique that can consistently discover messages concealed in WAV records. This is performed by accomplishing a four-layer 1-Dimensioal wavelet decay of the audio signals, applying support vector machines (SVMs) approach to identify the presence of concealed messages because of its excellent performance. Ru and his colleagues utilized a group of audios contain both of non-stego ones and stego ones as the learning and testing statistics to create the SVM categorizer. SVM is depends on Vapnik's geometric learning scheme (Vapnik, 1995). It generates a high border hyper plane that discrete the training vectors from diverse classes. When the border is full-sized, the probabilistic test fault range is un-maximized. Non-linear categorizer can be generated by way of mapping the primary entrance space into an upper dimensional characteristic space using a non-linear core task.

In (Kraetzer & Dittmann, 2007), the authors presented a method in audio steganalysis with a huge of information hiding processes is directed. The employed learned and tested recognizer method, utilizing a support vector machine (SVM) approach depends classification of characteristic collections produced by fusion both by Mel-Cepstral and time scope features, is assessed for its value as a kind of steganalysis method like as universal steganalysis implement as like as used another kind of steganalysis method like as specific steganalysis implement for voice over internet protocol (VoIP) steganography.

In (Qiao et al, 2009), a support vector machine (SVM) approach is used for diverse feature collections for classification and pattern inquiry. In (Liu et al, 2009), the authors applied a support vector machine (SVM) to distinguish the features of transferring stego -signals from non-stego-signals.

5.2 Data mining techniques on steganalysis over Text

In (Zhao et al, 2009), the authors proposed a novel steganalysis technique to discover the presence of concealed data utilizing feature replacement in contexts. This is performed by the use of SVM (Support Vector Machine) technique as a classifier to categorize the feature vector entrance into SVM. In the suggested discovery process, the purpose of SVM is to categorize feature vector, in order to separate normal (non stego) texts from stego (non-clear) texts. Depend on measurement training principle of VC–D and operational hazard minimization danger in (Chang and Lin, 2001), SVM is better than another method to answering ML (machine learning) problematic in a formal of non-big models, refining simplification acts, answering nonlinear and the most-D (dimensional) problems, etc. The discovery process can be partitioned into two portions. The first one is the training method and the second one is the classification method.

In (Chen et al, 2011), the authors provided a novel steganalysis scheme in contrast with replacement-based verbal steganography based on text suitable and declared how to utilize the measurements of text suitable values to differentiate among non-stego from stego texts. Also presented the SVM approach as a classifier besides the learning and testing corpus that needs two text groups named SVM training text group and SVM testing text group, both of that have subsections entitled non-stego and stego text.

5.3 Data mining techniques on steganalysis over Video

In (Kancherla & Mukkamala, 2009a, 2009b), the authors suggested a video steganalysis technique utilizing neural networks (NN) approach and support vector machines (SVM) approach to discover concealed data by investigating both the temporal redundancies and spatial redundancies. In their model supposed the non-stego video and the concealed data are not dependent and utilizes the probability quantity function of the inter-frame diversion signal to show the labelling influence caused by embedding files. In (Liu et al, 2008), presented an inter-frame correlation based on compacted video steganalysis techniques, applies collusion to the main feature from like video frames of a solo scene, and utilizes the blind classifier using a feed forward neural network (NN) abilitiy of non-linear character mapping.

5.4 Data mining techniques on steganalysis over Protocol

In (Huang et al, 2011), the authors presented a different steganalysis technique that uses regression investigation and the second discovery. The suggested technique not only can identify the concealed message imbedded in a compacted VoIP (voice over Internet protocol), but also precisely estimate the imbedded message length. The suggested technique depends on the second measurements, i.e. Performing a second steganography (imbedding data in an instant speech at an imbedding ratio tracked by imbedding extra data at a diverse layer of data imbedding) so as to estimate the concealed message length. Several repetitive trains were performed, in order to permit the establishment of the arithmetic relation between the imbedding rate and the rate of frequency point. Regression investigation was selected to try to find for the arithmetic rule, i.e. A numerical between the imbedding rate and the rate of frequency point, as exposed in (1)

$$T = e_0 + e_1 n + e_2 n^2 + e_3 n^3 \tag{1}$$

Where T is the imbedding ratio, n is rated of the frequency point of the sequence Z and e_0, e_1, e_2 and e_3 are the coefficients.

6. Discussion and analysis

In this section, the survey brief indicates that steganalysis with employed data mining techniques evaluate over Image, Audio, Text, Video and Protocol. It also Shows several graphs, figures and tables about performance and evaluates data mining techniques.

In fig. 3. We show a number of employed papers on data mining techniques on steganalysis based on discrimination of years corresponding to fig. 3. To have general survey of data mining techniques on steganalysis in this book chapter, it illustrates that this issue before than 15 years ago is important and this issue recently got more important than before and the number of research papers has been increased considerably.

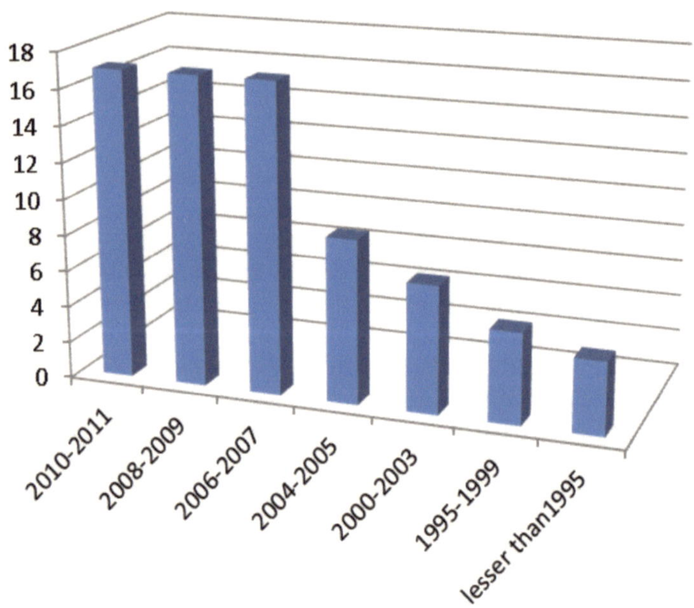

Fig. 3. Variety of employed Paper of data mining techniques on steganalysis.

Besides, in fig. 4. We have presented domain categorization based on recently published papers. It shows that image domain has the most extra spread domain (the first) and text domain is the least spread domain (the fourth).

We have another figure which indicates that data mining techniques have been used. In this figure (fig. 5) 75% of research works are devoted to classification problems, the rest (i.e. 25%) includes 12% deals with regression problems, 9% relate to clustering problems and the remained 4% relate to other problems.

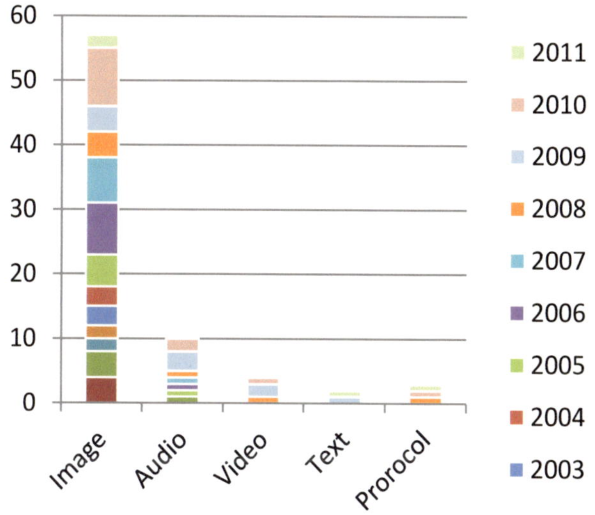

Fig.4. A glance of general categorization data mining techniques in steganalysis domain.

In fig. 5, by using kind of bar plot, we are going to show the rate of papers approximately in the scope of data mining techniques on steganalysis. It illustrates that SVM as one of classification techniques has involved maximum number of papers and also DT and KNN as a kind of classification techniques and cluster techniques which have involved a minimum number of papers.

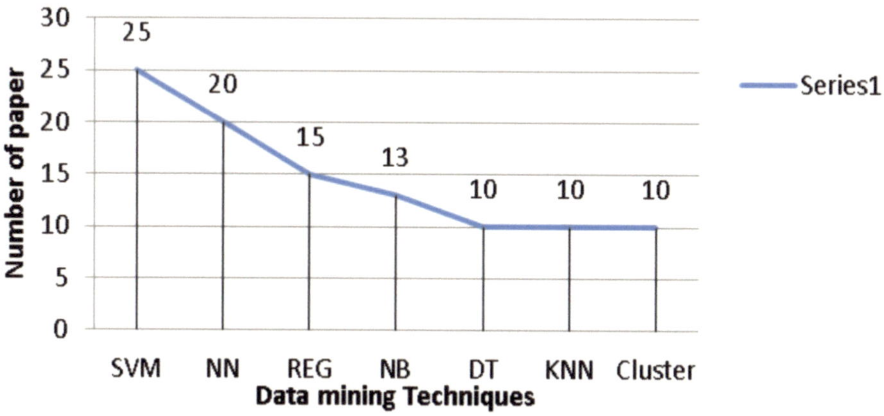

Fig.5. A parallel plot of variety of employed Paper of data mining techniques on steganalysis.

Fig. 6. Shows a parallel plot of the variety of employed papers of data mining techniques on steganalysis. According to this figure we can see that classification is the most important task in data mining which has been focused by researchers in steganalysis field.

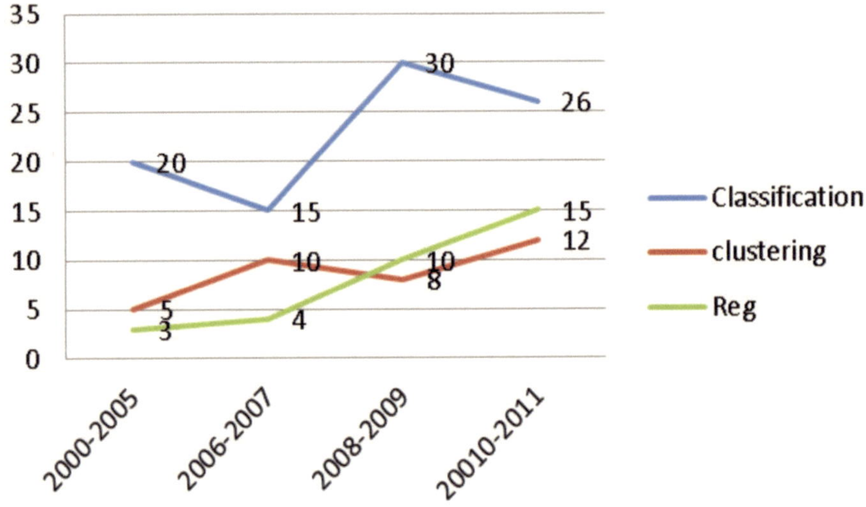

Fig. 6. A parallel plot of variety of employed papers of data mining techniques on steganalysis.

According to fig. 7. Classification approach consists 75% of overall approaches that the most technique was used, for this reason we intend declare in fig. 8 Classification methods that involves of: support vector machine (SVM), neural network (NN), K nearest neighbour (KNN), naive Bayes (NB) and decision tree (DT) approaches.

Fig.8. Shows that 46% of overall classification methods is SVM, 27% is related to NN, 11% to NB, 11% to DT and 5% to KNN.

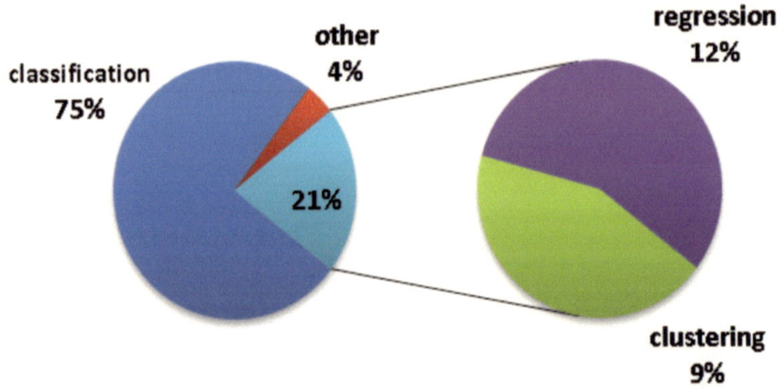

Fig. 7. Distribution of used data mining techniques.

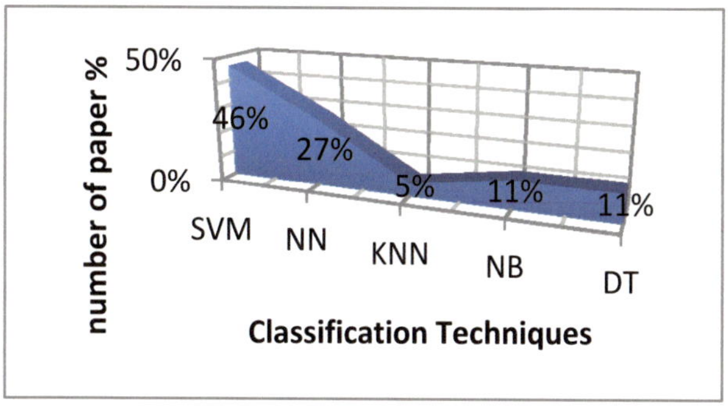

Fig. 8. Type of classification techniques.

Each method has its own self features and utilizes special data set and depends on diverse formats, thus in Table 1 we have a goal to review four new nested approaches that used the second detection method. Second detection is the newest method in steganalysis that performs after hiding message detection or discrimination of stego file from the non - stego file. This method depends on dynamic steganalysis problems that consist of estimate length of concealed message, detect security key stego files, estimate amount of MPVD and etc.

Paper	Feature	DM Technique	Type of steganalysis	Domain	First detection	Second detection
Steganalysis of compressed speech to detect covert voice over Internet protocol channels		Regression	Static, Dynamic	Protocol	Discover embeds message	Length of concealing message
Message estimation for universal steganalysis using multi-classification support vector machine		SVM	Static, Dynamic	Image	Stego/ clear image	Length of concealing message
Steganalysis of HMPD reversible data hiding scheme		SVM	Static, Dynamic	Image	Stego / clear image	Security key stego
Steganalysis and payload estimation of embedding in pixel differences using neural networks		Neural Networks (NN)	Static, Dynamic	Image	Stego / clear image	MPVD

Table 1. A Brief review of four new nested methods.

In table 2, we show some data sets that used in the papers; they are different with each other so we can't compare them. There were seldom featured vectors in papers therefore table 3 just shows three feature vectors.

No	Paper	Data set
1	(Yang et al, 2011)	Downloaded 3000 originally very high resolution color images in format "tiff" from http://photogallery.nrcs.usda.gov, and partitioned them into 15 groups averagely
2	(Davidson et al, 2005)	There are total of 1300 images, which had been cleared of copyright issues. (http://www.datahiding.org), courtesy of Dr. Edward Delp, Purdue University
3	(Tan et al, 2006)	Three hundred images are randomly selected from human, architecture and landscape categories of photo.net image database, one hundred images from each category.
4	(Zhou et al, 2010), (Kobsi& Merouani, 2007)	1096 sample images CorelDraw image database. Included in the CorelDRAW (www.corel.com).
5	(Chou et al, 2010)	The uncompressed color image database (UCID) consists of 1338 was used as the cover images in the training set. The INRIA Holidays dataset has 1491 images was used for the cover images in the testing set.
6	(Michael et al, 2006)	Set of 5075 images from 5 different digital cameras (all over 4 megapixels).
7	(Xuan et al, 2007)	1096 BMP images with size of 768x512 in the CorelDraw-www.corel.com
8	(Liu & H. Sung, 2007)	5000 TIFF raw format digital pictures from Olympus C740. These images are 24-bit, 640*480 pixels, lossless true color and never compressed
9	(Miche et al, 2007)	13 000 images of natural scenes, coming from 5 different digital cameras.
10	(Liu et al, 2006)	The original images in our experiments are 5000 TIFF raw format digital pictures from Olympus C740, taken in U.S.A, across spring to winter.
11	(Liua et al, 2008)	The original images in our experiments are 5000 TIFF raw format digital pictures, taken in USA during 2003–2005.
12	(Mehrabi et al, 2007)	860 gray levels PGM images.
13	(Sajedi & Jamzad , 2008)	Used 315 images randomly selected from Washington university image database http://www.cs.washington.edu/research/image database
14	(Joo et al , 2010)	2000 color images from the USDA NRCS Photo Gallery
15	(Lou et al , 2009)	860 color images in JPEG format from content based image Retrieval (CBIR) University of Washington, July 30 2007 http://www.cs.washington.edu/research/imagedatabase/groundtruth
16	(Cho et al, 2010)	Among these 3580 images, 570 images were randomly downloaded from the image database
17	(Qiao et al, 2009)	The dataset contains 1000 mono MP3 audio files with the bit rate of 128 kbps and the sample rate of 44 KHz. Each audio has the duration of 18 seconds

18	(Liu et al, 2009)	1000 WAV audio signals files covering different types such as digital speech, on-line broadcast, and music, etc.
19	(Zou et al, 2006)	Used 2812 images download from the website of Vision Research Lab, University of California, Santa Barbara.

Table 2. The list of different used Date sets.

No	Paper	Feature vector
1	(Gujar Madhavan, 2006)	There are 9 feature vector that includes: $\mu_1(W)=\sum_{k=1}^{4}(\max(f(k,j))-\min(f(k,j)))2^{4(k+1)}$ $\mu_2(W)=\sum 2^{C_i}L_i$ $\mu_3(W)=2^{\#1(b_0)}+2^{\#1(b_0+b_1)}+2^{\#1(b_1+b_2)}+2^{\#1(b_2+b_3)}$ $\mu_4(W)=(\sum_{k=0}^{31}\lvert f_j\rvert^2)^{1/2}$ $\mu 5$ (W) = Weighted Hadamard transform. Using an 8x8 Hadamard matrix (H) and the operation y = Hx $\mu 6(W)$, $\mu 7(W)$, $\mu 8(W)$, $\mu 9(W)=\sum p_j \log p_j$
2	(Geetha et al, 2010)	$F=(f_1^P, f_2^P,\ldots f_5^P, f_1^P, f_2^{P+1},\ldots f_5^{P+1}, \ldots,f_1^{P+4}, f_2^{P+4}, \ldots, f5^{P+4},Type)$
3	(Zhou et al, 2010)	$F_{xb}(U,V,C)=J_{m(U,V)}/N^*(\min\lvert v_i-v_j\rvert^2)$

Table 3. The list of used feature vectors.

7. Conclusion and future work

In this book chapter, we have proposed a survey for data mining techniques on steganalysis. As it was mentioned in the presented chapter, different medias have been used as the cover media such as: image, audio, text, protocol and video. This survey has reviewed several published data mining techniques for steganalysis. We showed that SVM, as a type of classification method, got the best results in comparison to other classification techniques.

The future work in steganalysis would be the employment of advanced bio-inspired metaheuristic algorithms, such as Genetic Algorithms, Ant Colony Optimization, Particle Swarm Optimization and Artificial Immune Systems, to construct efficient learning classifier systems. This employment enables us to explore the huge search space more efficiently and discover more accurate steganalysis knowledge.

8. Reference

Avcibas, I. and Memon, N. and Sankur, B. (2002). Image steganalysis with binary similarity measures, *Image Processing. 2002. Proceedings. 2002 International Conference on,* Vol. 3, no., pp. 645- 648, ISBN: 0-7803-7622- June 2002.

Avcıbas, I and Memon, N and Sankur, B.(2003). Steganalysis Using Image Quality Metrics, *ieee transactions on image processing,* VOL. 12, NO. 2, pp.221-229

Avcibas, I.(2006). Audio steganalysis with content-independent distortion measures, *Signal Processing Letters, IEEE,* vol.13, no.2, pp. 92- 95, ISSN : 1070-9908, Feb. 2006

Baragada, S.R. and Ramakrishna, S. and Rao, MS and Purushothaman, S.(2008). Implementation of Radial Basis Function Neural Network for Image Steganalysis, *International Journal of Computer Science and Security (IJCSS)*, Vol.2, No.1, pp.12-22, ISSN : 1985-1553.

Benton, R. and Chu, H. (2005). Soft Computing Approach to Steganalysis of LSB Embedding in Digital Images, *Information Technology: Research and Education, 2005. ITRE 2005. 3rd International Conference on*, pp.105-109, ISBN: 0-7803-8932-8, June2005

Berg, G. and Davidson, I. and Duan, M.Y. and Paul, G. (2003). Searching For Hidden Messages: Automatic Detection of Steganography, *Proceedings of the 15th Innovative Applications of AI Conference*, pp.51-56, August, 2003, Acapulco, Mexico.

Bhatt, C.A. and Kankanhalli, M.S.(2011). Multimedia data mining: state of the art and challenges, *Multimedia Tools and Application*, Vol.51, No.1, pp.35-76.

Chen, C. and Shi, Y.Q. and Chen, W. and Xuan, G. (2006). statistical moments based universal steganalysis using jpeg 2-d array and 2-d characteristic function, *Image Processing, 2006 IEEE International Conference on*, Vol.6, ISBN: 1-4244-0481-9 pp.105-108, Atlanta, GA, USA

Chen, Z. and Huang, Land Miao, H. and Yang, W. and Meng, P. (2011).Steganalysis against substitution-based linguistic steganography based on context clusters, *Computer and Electrical Engineering*, Vol.37, No.6, pp.1071-1081, ISSN = 0045-7906.June 2011

Cho, S. and Wang, J. and Kuo, C.C.J. and Cha, B.H. (2010). BLOCK-BASED IMAGE STEGANALYSIS FOR A MULTI-CLASSIFIER, *Multimedia and Expo (ICME), 2010 IEEE International Conference on*, Vol.0, pp.1457-1462, ISBN: 978-1-4244-7491-2 July 2010, Singapore,

Cortes, C and Vapnik, V. (1995) Support-vector networks, *in Machine Learning*, Vol.20, No.3, pp. 273-297, ISSN: 0885-6125.

Davidson, J. and Bergman, C. and Bartlett, E. (2005). An artificial neural network for wavelet steganalysis, *Proceedings of SPIE - The International Society for Optical Engineering, Mathematical Methods in Pattern and Image Analysis,*, vol. 5916, pp. 1-10. ISBN 0-8194-5921-6, August 2005, San Diego, California, USA.

Geetha, S. and Ishwarya, N. and Kamaraj, N. (2010).Audio steganalysis with Hausdorff distance higher order statistics using a rule based decision tree paradigm .*Expert Systems with Applications*, Vol.37, No.12, pp. 7469-7482, ISSN 0957-4174

Guorong, X and Xia, C and Shi, Y.Q. and Wen, C and Xuefeng, T and Cong, H.(2007).JPEG Steganalysis Based on Classwise Non-Principal Components Analysis and Multi-Directional Markov Model, *Multimedia and Expo, 2007 IEEE International Conference on*, pp.903-906, ISBN : 1-4244-1017-7, Beijing, July 2007.

Huang, Y. and Tang, S. and Bao, C. and Yip, Y.J.(2011). Steganalysis of compressed speech to detect covert voice over Internet protocol channels, *Information Security, IET*, vol.5, no.1, pp.26-32, ISSN: 1751-8709.

Holoska, J, Oplatkova, Z, Zelinka, I and Senkerik, R (2010).Comparison Between Neural Network Steganalysis And Linear Classification Method Stegdetect, *Computational Intelligence, Modeling and Simulation (CIMSiM), 2010 Second International Conference on, .Vol.10, pp.*15-20, ISBN: 978-0-7695-4262-1, Sept. 2010, Bali

Joo, J.C. and Oh, T.W. and Choi, J.H. and Lee, H.K. (2010). Steganalysis scheme using the difference image of calibrated sub-sampling, *Intelligent Information Hiding and*

Multimedia Signal Processing (IIH-MSP), 2010 Sixth International Conference on, pp.51-54, ISBN : 978-0-7695-4222-5, Darmstadt, Oct. 2010

Kaipa, B. and Robila, S.A.. (2010). Statistical Steganalyis of Images Using Open Source Software, *Applications and Technology Conference (LISAT), 2010 Long Island Systems,* pp.1-5, ISBN: 978-1-4244-5550-8, May 2010, Farmingdale, NY

Kancherla, K.; Mukkamala, S.(2009).Video steganalysis using motion estimation, *Neural Networks, 2009. IJCNN 2009. International Joint Conference on.,* pp.1510-1515, ISBN : 978-1-4244-3549-4, Atlanta, GA June 2009.

Ker, A.D. and Pevny, T. (2011). A New Paradigm for Steganalysisvia Clustering. *Proc. SPIE Media Watermarking, Security, and Forensics XIII,* Vol.7880, pp. 78800U-78813U, Bellingham, ISBN 978-0-8194-8417-8.

KOBSI, N. and MEROUANI, H.F. (2007). Neural Network Based Image Steganalysis: A Comparative Study, *Neural Networks for Signal Processing [1994] IV. Proceedings of the 1994 IEEE Workshop,* pp:423-430, ISBN: 0-7803-2026-3, Sep 1994, Ermioni,

Kodovský, J and Fridrich, J.(2012). Ensemble Classifiers for Steganalysis of Digital Media, *ieee transactions on information forensics and security,* VOL. 7, NO. 2, pp.432-444, ISBN: 1556-6013

Kraetzer, C. and Dittmann, J. (2007). Pros and Cons of Mel-cepstrum based Audio Steganalysis using SVM Classification, *Proceedings of the 9th international conference on Information hiding,* Vol., No., pp.359-377, ISBN: 978-3-540-77369-6, June, 2007, Saint Malo, France

Kraetzer, C. and Dittmann, J.(2008). Cover Signal Specific Steganalysis: the Impact of Training on the Example of two Selected Audio Steganalysis Approaches, *Proceedings of the Electronic Imaging Conf. on Security, Forensics, Steganography, and Watermarking of Multimedia Contents,* Vol. 6819.

Kraetzer, C. and Dittmann, J.(2009). The impact of information fusion in steganalysis on the example of audio steganalysis. *Proceedings of the Media Forensics and Security XI. Electronic Imaging Conference,* Vol.7254, ISBN 9780819475046, February 2009

Kraetzer, C. and Oermann, A. and Dittmann, J. and Lang, A. (2007). Digital Audio Forensics: A First Practical Evaluation on Microphone and Environment Classification, *Proceedings of the 9th workshop on Multimedia & security,* pp.63-74, ISBN: 978-1-59593-857-2, New York, NY, USA

Laxman, S. and Sastry, P.S.(2006). A survey of temporal data mining, Sadhana, *Academy Proceedings in Engineering Sciences,* Vol.31, No.2, pp.173-198,

Lin, E. and Woertz, E. and Kam, M.(2004). LSB steganalysis using support vector regression, *Information Assurance Workshop, 2004. Proceedings from the Fifth Annual IEEE SMC.,* pp.95-100, June 2004, ISBN:0-7803-8572-1

Liu, Q. and Sung, A. and Qiao, M.(2009).Spectrum steganalysis of WAV audio streams, *Machine Learning and Data Mining in Pattern Recognition,* Vol. 5632, pp. 582-593, ISBN:978-3-642-03070-3-44. Berlin Heidelberg 2009

Liu, Q. and Sung, A.H. (2007). Feature Mining and Neuro-Fuzzy Inference System for Steganalysis of LSB Matching Stegangoraphy in Grayscale Images, *Proceedings of the 20th international joint conference on Artifical intelligence,* pp.2808-2813, January, 2007, Hyderabad, India

Liu, Q. and Sung, A.H. and Chen, Z. and Xu, J. (2008). Feature mining and pattern classification for steganalysis of LSBmatching steganography in grayscale images, *Pattern Recognition,* Vol.41, No.1, pp.56-66, ISSN: 00313203

Liu, Q. and Sung, A.H. and Xu, J. and Ribeiro, B.M. (2006). Image Complexity and Feature Extraction for Steganalysis of LSB Matching Steganography, *Pattern Recognition, 2006. ICPR 2006. 18th International Conference on,* Vol.2, pp.267-270, ISBN:0-7695-2521-0, Hong Kong September 2006

Liu, Q. and Sung, A.H.(2007).Feature mining and nuero-fuzzy inference system for steganalysis of LSB matching steganography in gray scale images, *Proceedings of the 20th international joint conference on Artificial intelligence,* pp.2808-2813, Hyderabad, India, January

Liu, S. and Yao, H. and Gao, W. (2004).Steganalysis Based on Wavelet Texture Analysis and Neural Network, *Intelligent Control and Automation, 2004. WCICA 2004. Fifth World Congress on,* Vol.5, pp.4066--4069

Lopez-Hernandez, J. and Martinez-Noriega, R. and Nakano-Miyatake, M. and Yamaguchi, K. (2008).Detection of BPCS-steganography using SMWCF steganalysis and SVM, *Information Theory and Its Applications, 2008.ISITA 2008. International Symposium on,* pp.1-5, ISBN: 978-1-4244-2069-8 Dec. 2008

Lou, D.C. and Hu, C.H. and Chou, C.L. and Chiu, C.C. (2011). Steganalysis of HMPD reversible data hiding scheme, *Optics Communications*(June 2011), Vol.284, pp.5406-5414, ISSN:0030-4018

Lou, D.C. and Liu, C.L. and Lin, C.L. (2009).Message estimation for universal steganalysis using multi-classification support vector machine, *Computer Standards& Interfaces,* Vol.31, No.2, (March 2008)pp.420-427, ISSN: 0920-5489

Lyu, S. and Farid, H. (2004). Steganalysis Using Color Wavelet Statistics and One-Class Support Vector Machines, *SPIE Symposium on Electronic Imaging,* Vol.5306, pp35-46, ISBN : 0-8194-5209-2, San Jose CA, USA, April 2004

Marvel, L. and Henz, B. and Boncelet, C. (2008). Fusing Rate-Specific SVM Classifiers for ±1 Embedding Steganalysis, *Information Sciences and Systems, 2008. CISS 2008. 42nd Annual Conference on,* vol., no., pp.361-364, ISBN: 978-1-4244-2247-0, Princeton, NJ, March 2008.

Meghanathan, N and Nayak, L.(2010).steganalysis algorithms for detecting the hidden information in image, audio and video cover media, *International Journal of Network Security & Its Application (IJNSA),* Vol.2, No.1, ISSN: 0975- 2307

Mehrabi, M.A. and Faez, K. and Bayesteh, A.R. (2007). Image Steganalysis Based on Statistical Moments of Wavelet Subband Histograms in Different Frequencies and Support Vector Machine, *Natural Computation, 2007. ICNC 2007. Third International Conference on,* Vol.1, pp.587-590, ISBN: 0-7695-2875-9, Aug. 2007.

Miche, Y. and Bas, P. and Lendasse, A. and Jutten, C. and Simula, O. (2007). Advantages of Using Feature Selection Techniques on Steganalysis Schemes, *Computational and Ambient Intelligence,* pp.606-613, ISBN: 978-3-540-73006-4,

Miche, Y. and Roue, B. and Lendasse, A. and Bas, P. (2006).A Feature Selection Methodology for Steganalysis, *Multimedia Content Representation, Classification and Security,* pp.49-56, ISBN = 3-540-39392-7, 978-3-540-39392-4, Istanbul, Turkey,

Nissar, A. and Mir, A.H.(2010). Classification of steganalysis techniques A study, *Digital Signal Processing,* Vol.20, No.6, pp.1758-1770, ISSN 1051-2004

Qiao, M. and Sung, A.H. and Liu, Q.(2009).Steganalysis of mp3stego, *Neural Networks, 2009. IJCNN 2009. International Joint Conference on,* pp.2566-2571, ISSN: 1098-7576, Atlanta, GA, June 2009

Rodriguez, B.M. and Peterson, G.L. and Bauer, K.W. and Agaian, S.S..(2006). Steganalysis Embedding Percentage Determination with Learning Vector Quantization. *systems, Man and Cybernetics, 2006. SMC'06. IEEE International Conference on,* V. 3, pp 1861-1865, ISBN: 1424400996

Ru, X.M. and Zhang, H.J. and Huang, X.(2005) Steganalysis of audio: Attacking the steghide, *Machine Learning and Cybernetics, 2005. Proceedings of 2005 International Conference on,* Vol.7, pp.3937-3942, ISBN: 0-7803-9091-1, Aug. 2005

Sabeti, V. and Samavi, S. and Mahdavi, M. and Shirani, S. (2009).Steganalysis of Embedding in Divergence of Image Pixel Pairs by Neural Network, *the ISC Intel Journal of Information Security ISeCure,* Vol.1, No.1, pp.17-26, ISSN: 2008-2045

Sabeti, V. and Samavi, S. and Mahdavi, M. and Shirani, S. (2010). Steganalysis and payload estimation of embedding in pixel differences using neural Networks, *Pattern Recognition,* Vol.43, No.1, pp.405-415, ISSN: 0031-3203,

Sajedi, H and Jamzad, M.(2008). A Steganalysis Method Based on Contourlet Transform Coefficients, *Intelligent Information Hiding and Multimedia Signal Processing, 2008. IIHMSP '08 International Conference on,* pp.245-248, ISBN: 978-0-7695-3278-3, Aug. 2008

Shaohui, L. and Hongxun, Y. and Wen, G. (2003). neural network based steganalysis in still images, *Proceedings of the 2003 International Conference on Multimedia and Expo,* Vol.1, pp.509-512, ISBN:0-7803-7965-9, July, 2003

Shi, Y.Q. and Xuan, G. and Zou, D. and Gao, J. and Yang, C. and Zhang, Z. and Chai, P. and Chen, W. and Chen, C. (2005). Image Steganalysis Based on Moments of Characteristic Functions Using Wavelet Decomposition, Prediction-Error Image, and Neural Network, *ICME(ICMCS) - International Conference on Multimedia Computing and Systems/ International Conference on Multimedia and Expo,* pp. 269-272, July 2005, ISBN: 0-7803-9332-5

Tan, S. and Huang, J. and Yang, Z. and Shi, Y.Q. (2006). steganalysis of jpeg2000 lazy-mode steganography using the hilbert-huang transform based sequential analysis hilbert-huang transform based sequential analysis, *Image Processing, IEEE International Conference on,* Vol.0, pp.101-104, Oct. 2006. Atlanta, GA, ISSN: 1522-4880.

Tuia, D. and Kanevski, M. and Munoz Mari, J. and Camps-Valls, G. (2010). cluster-based active learning for compact image classification, *Geoscience and Remote Sensing Symposium (IGARSS), 2010 IEEE International,* Vol., pp.2824-2827, ISSN : 2153-6996, Honolulu, HI, July 2010.

Xiao, Y.Y and Aiming, W.(2009).An Investigation of Genetic Algorithm on Steganalysis Techniques, Intelligent *Information Hiding and Multimedia Signal Processing, 2009. IIH-MSP '09. Fifth International Conference on,* pp.1118-1121, ISBN : 978-0-7695-3762-7, Kyoto, Sept. 2009.

Xiao.Y. Y and Aiming W. (2009).Steganalysis Based on Regression Model and Bayesion Network, *Multimedia Information Networking and Security, 2009. MINES '09. International Conference on,* vol.1, pp.41-44, ISBN: 978-1-4244-5068-8, Hubei, Nov. 2009

Xuan, G. and Shi, Y. and Huang, C. and Fu, D. and Zhu, X. and Chai, P. and Gao, J. (2006). Steganalysis using high-dimensional features derived from co-occurrence matrix and class-wise non-principal components analysis (CNPCA), *Proceedings of the 5th international conference on Digital Watermarking*, pp.49-60, ISBN: 3-540-48825-1, 978-3-540-48825-5, Jeju Island, Korea, 2006

Yang, C. and Liu, F. and Luo, X (2011). Error Correction of Sample Pair Analysis Based on Support Vector Regression, *Multimedia Information Networking and Security (MINES), 2011 Third International Conference on*, pp.633-636 Shanghai, Nov, 2011, ISBN: 978-0-7695-4559-2

Zhao, X and Huang, L. and Li, L. and Yang, W. and Chen, Z. and Yu, Z. (2009). Steganalysis on Character Substitution Using Support Vector Machine, *Proceedings of the 2009 Second International Workshop on Knowledge Discovery and Data Mining*, No.5, pp.84-88, ISBN:978-0-7695-3543-2, Moscow, Jan. 2009

Zhou, Z, Zhang, X, Chen, Z. (2010). A Universal Steganalysis Based on One-Class Classification, *Journal of Computational Information Systems*, VOl.6, No.9, pp.2941-2948, ISBN: 1553-9105

Zou, D. and Shi, Y.Q. and Su, W. and Xuan, G. (2006). Steganalysis Based on Markov Model of Thresholded Prediction-Error Image, *Multimedia and Expo, 2006 IEEE International Conference on (ICME)*, Vol.6, pp.1365-1368, ISBN: 1-4244-0367-7, July, 2006, Toronto

2

Steganography in Different Colour Models Using an Energy Adjustment Applying Wavelets

Blanca E. Carvajal-Gámez, Francisco J. Gallegos-Funes, Alberto J. Rosales-Silva and Rene Santiago-Cruz
National Polytechnic Institute,
Higher School of Mechanical and Electrical Engineering,
Edif. Z-4, 3er. Piso, ESIME SEPI-Electrónica, Col. Lindavista, México DF.,
México

1. Introduction

The information concealment concerns to the process of integrating information or data elements into music, video, and images (Chia- Chen et al. 2008). The hidden information in steganography does not have relationship with the host image. The information contained in the host image is just a distraction to the receiver, so this is of no so much interest in its full recovery, but the host image must have the minimum quality, considered because any relief, color or misplaced pixels can cause some suspicion and is susceptible to extract the hidden information without authorization from the transmitter. The most important is the hidden information, which must have a full recovery.

Steganography in our days performs vital importance since it is a support tool to the copyright protection, which the authentication processes allow the distribution and legal use of different material.

Due to rapid growth of the computer hardware, several developing mediums such as e-books, i-tunes, etc., make possible to request in an economic and rapid way the copy of audio, image, or video file. From this point of view, there arises the need of copy protection systems to use and distribute different material in a legal way. Therefore, several steganographic methods have been proposed, which are effective and secure in the transmission or copying of information because these are based on half visibly innocent as a carrier of information and only with a key or password can access to hidden information inserted. This information does not substantially alter the host image, however, is susceptible to Human Vision System (HVS) (Wang- Zhou et al. 2002). The host image with the hidden information is known as stego-image. Typically, there are two techniques to realize a stego-image: in the space domain and frequency domain. The most common method for space domain is the Last Significant Bit (LSB), which is the modification of the least significant bit in each pixel of the image (Chung-Ming et al. 2008). In the Frequency Domain, the Discrete Fourier Transform (DFT), the Discrete Cosine Transform (DCT), and

Discrete Wavelet Transform (DWT) are used to transform the spatial pixel values in frequency coefficients (Yuan-Hui et al. 2005). A number of factors cause in an edge some sensitivity to the human eye and the noise effects of noise in the human eye as the luminance, frequency band, and texture. The human eye is less sensitive to noise in high frequency sub band (Reddy – A.A. et al. 2005). The sensitivity to noise of the human eye in the textures that conforms an image is less if is closer to the edges. Based on these observations, an adaptable model for image compression using wave coefficients quantization was developed (Reddy – A.A. et al. 2005). A method was developed using a concealment function to compute the weight factors into the pseudo random binary sequence in the high frequency components of the host image (Reddy – A.A. et al. 2005).

In this paper, we use the steganographic method implemented in (Carvajal - Gamez et al. 2008) with some modifications. A scaling factor depending directly on the number of bits of the host image is proposed to ensure that with the use of steganographic technique does not affect the host image and the hidden information is not visible to the HVS. Applying the scaling factor the energy generated by the host image is preserved to approximate the original image, eliminating any visual disturbance, being imperceptible to the human eye.

2. Proposed method

Proposed steganographic algorithm is based on the DWT (Carvajal – Gamez, 2008; Kutter, 1999). The image resolution applying DWT is divided into 4 submatrices called approximations **a**, horizontal **h**, vertical **v**, and diagonal **d**, see Figure 1. Each submatrix is a copy of the original image but in different frequency level which provides a certain amount of energy (Moon ,2007; Walker, 2003). In this image subdivision the steganographic algorithm is applied only in the submatrix **h** and the other ones are discarded. The proposed steganographic algorithm based on wavelets is shown in Figure 2 (Carvajal – Gamez et al. 2008). The second block of Figure 2 refers to the double decomposition wavelet applied to the hide image and a simple decomposition wavelet to the host image. Having obtained 4 submatrices **a**, **h**, **v**, and **d**, we choose the submatrix **h** to perform the hiding, that is because it contains the edges of the image, known as wavelet components of low-high frequencies. This election is because the edges are considered natural noisy areas which are suitable to hide. Later for the hidden image there is elected the submatrix **a** which consists of the components wavelets which contribute 90 % of entire energy of the image. The third block refers to obtaining the standard deviation σ_R, with it to apply the following criterion of insertion: $\sigma_R \leq x[n/2, m/2]$ then $y[n,m]$, where $x[n, m]$ is the host image and $y[n, m]$ (see figure 2) is the hidden image. Finally, we perform the Inverse Discrete Wavelet Transform to obtain the modified image (with the host image inserted the hide image).

DWT is closely linked to the multi-resolution analysis, that is, the observation of the signal or the image at different frequencies (Vetterli M. et al. 1995), which allows a broader knowledge of the signal and facilitates the fast computation when the wavelet family is orthogonal (Carvajal - Gamez et al. 2008; Debnath, 2002; Petrosian et al. 2002; Vetterli et al. 2011). The wavelets Ψ can be obtained such that the family moved for j and dilated for n,

$$\left\{ \psi_{j,n}(t) = \frac{1}{\sqrt{2^j}} \psi\left(\frac{t \;\; 2^j n}{2^j} \right) \right\}_{j,n \in Z^2} \tag{1}$$

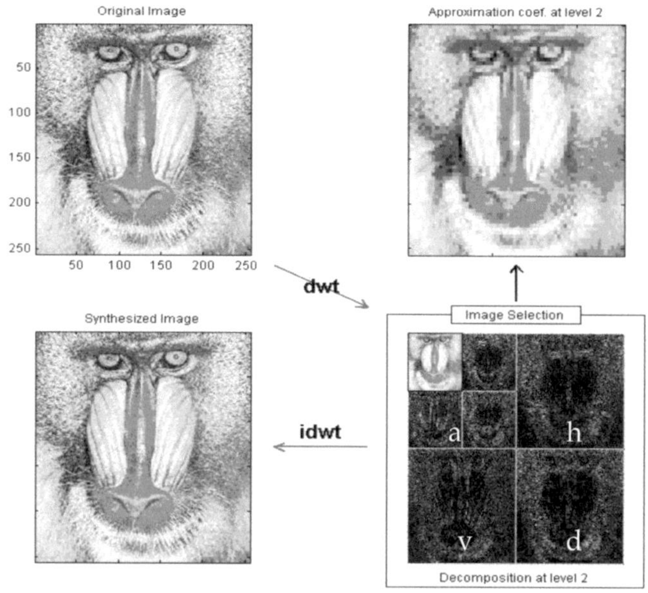

Fig 1. Two levels decomposition using DWT in the Mandrill image.

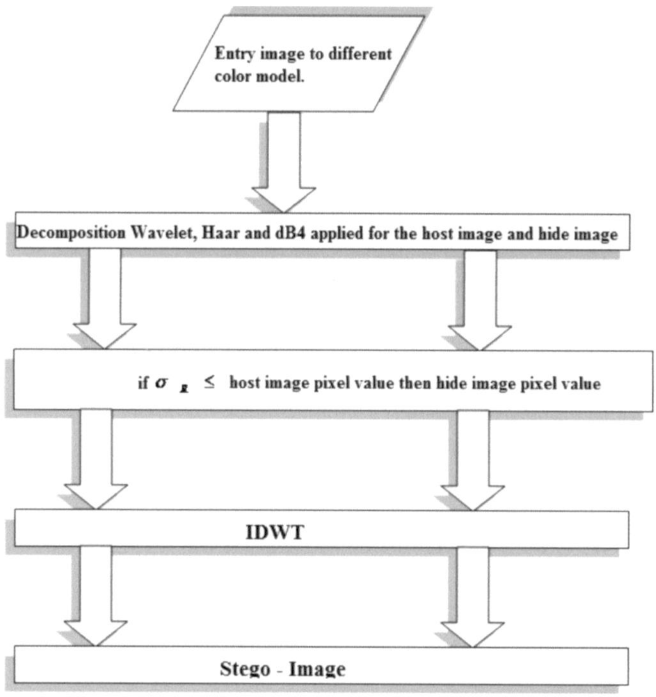

Fig 2. Block diagram of the steganographic algorithm.

it is a orthonormal base of $L^2(R)$ (Carvajal - Gamez et al. 2008; Debnath, 2002; Petrosian et al. 2002; Vetterli et al. 2011). These orthogonal wavelets transport information about the changes of the signal to the resolution 2^{-j}. Then, the analysis of multi-resolution appears: an image will be modeled with orthogonal projections on vector space of different resolution, $PV_jf, V_j \subset L^2(R)$ (Debnath, 2002; Vetterli et al. 2011). The quantity of information in every projection will depend on the size of the orthogonal projection V_j. The multi-resolution analysis calculates the approach of signals to different resolutions with orthogonal projections in spaces $\{V_j\}$.

Also, the multi-resolution approaches are characterized completely by a particular discrete filter that controls the loss of information along the different resolutions. The approach of a function f with a resolution 2^{-j} comes specified by a discrete sampling grid, which provides local averages of f in a neighborhood of proportional size to 2^j. This means that the approach of a function to a resolution 2^{-j} is defined as an orthogonal projection in a space $V_j \subset L^2(R)$ (Vetterli et al. 2011). The space V_j regroups all the possible approaches to the resolution 2^{-j}. We consider, in this study, that the resolution 2^{-j} corresponds with a scale 2^j. The orthonormal wavelets carry the necessary details to increase the resolution of the approach of the signal.

The function $f(t)$ can be reconstructed from the discrete wavelets coefficients $W_f(j,n)$ in the following way,

$$f(t) = A\sum_j \sum_n W_f(j,n)\psi_{j,n}(t), \tag{2}$$

where j is the scale factor, n is the movement factor and A is a constant that no depends on $f(t)$. The wavelets $\psi_{j,n}(t)$ generated of the same wavelet mother function $\psi(t)$ have different scale j and place n, but they have the same form. Scale factor $j>0$ is always used. The wavelet is dilated when the scale $j>1$, and it is contracted when $j<1$. This way, changing the value of j the different range from frequencies is covered. Big values of the parameter j correspond to frequencies of minor range, or a big scale of $\psi_{j,n}(t)$. Small values of j correspond to frequencies of minor range or a very small scale of $\psi_{j,n}(t)$ (Bogges A. et al. 2001; Sheng Y., 2002).The continuous wavelet functions with discrete factors of scale and movement are named discrete wavelets. Finally, the signal $f(t)$ can be compressed or expand in the time. This will have little certainly after effects in the plane of frequencies (Bogges A. et al. 2001),

$$\begin{aligned} &f(t) \textit{compression by a factor } 2^j (s) f_s(t) = \frac{1}{\sqrt{2^j}} f\left(\frac{t}{s}\right) \\ &\hat{f}(w) \textit{ compression by a factor } \frac{1}{2^j} \hat{f}_{2^j}(w) = \frac{1}{\sqrt{2^j}} 2^j \hat{f}\left(2^j w\right) = \sqrt{2^j}\,\hat{f}\left(2^j w\right) \end{aligned} \tag{3}$$

where $\hat{f}(w)$ represent the reconstruction of f(t).

The coefficient of the decomposition of a function f in an orthogonal base of wavelets is calculated by a subsequent algorithm of discrete convolution of h and g, and realizes a sampling of the eq. (4) and (5),

$$x_{low}[k] = \sum_n x[n,m]h[2k-l] \ , \tag{4}$$

$$x_{high}[k] = \sum_{n} x[n,m] g[2k-h] \,, \tag{5}$$

where $x[n,m]$ is an image, $x_{low}[k]$ and $x_{high}[k]$ are outputs of the Low Pass Filter (LPF) and High Pass Filter HPF respectively; $g[2k\text{-}l]$ and $h[2k\text{-}h]$ represent the impulse response of HPF and LPF, respectively, sub-sampled by a factor of 2 as expressed in eq. (4) and (5) (Vetterli et al. 1995). These coefficients $x_{low}[k]$ and $x_{high}[k]$ are calculated by cascades of discrete filters, through of convolution and sampling. The Figure 3 depicts this decomposition.

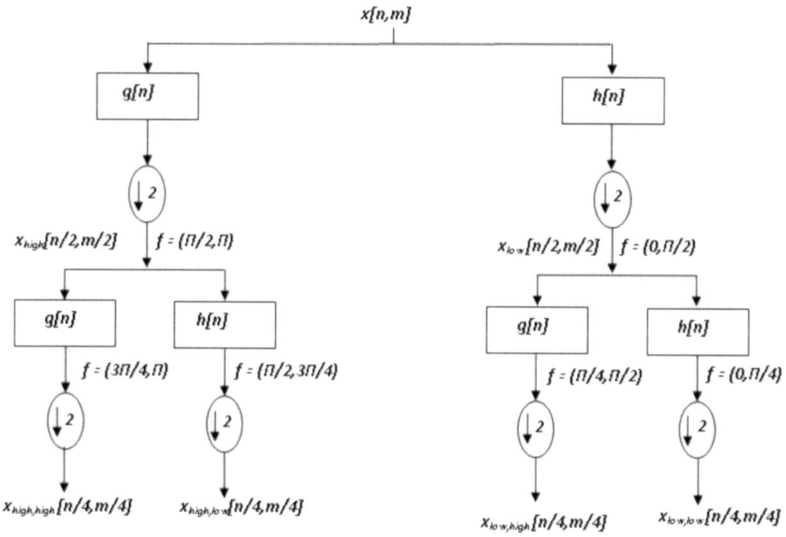

Fig. 3. Wavelet decomposition scheme.

In the case of images, the host image $x[n,m]$ must pass through a series of mirror filters banks in quadrature (Petrosian et al. 2002; Vetterli et al. 1995; Walker, 2003), these are Low Pass Filter (LPF) and High Pass Filter (HPF). The signal from each filter is decimated by a factor of 2. The filter h removes the components high-high and high-low frequencies of the $x[n,m]$, while g is a high-pass filter, which removes the components low-low and low-high frequencies. For the reconstruction, an interpolation is realized, inserting zeros and expanding $x_{high,high}$, $x_{high,low}$, $x_{low,high}$, $x_{low,low}$. This filtering and decimation process in a continuous way is known as sub-band coding. Figure 4 depicts the decomposition of the discrete wavelet for a RGB color image, it is interpreted as the decomposition of the submatrix **R** (representing the Red channel) represented by $X_R[n,m]$, for the first $X_R[n,m]$ decomposition shown in Figure 4 applies to itself step of the low-pass filter through the rows and columns to obtain submatrix **a** to previously mentioned of the image, in the second decomposition is applied the low-pass filtering through the rows and columns obtain the submatrix **h**, the third decomposition is similar to **h** but reverses the first filter is the high-pass filter and later the low-pass filter and get the sub matrix **v** and finally for submatrix **d** filtering is applied throught in rows and columns with the high-pass filter. The terms $h[m]$ or $h[n]$ and $g[m]$ or $g[n]$ represent the impulse response of the LPF and HPF respectively, xh and xg represent the sub images that are decimated by a factor of 2.

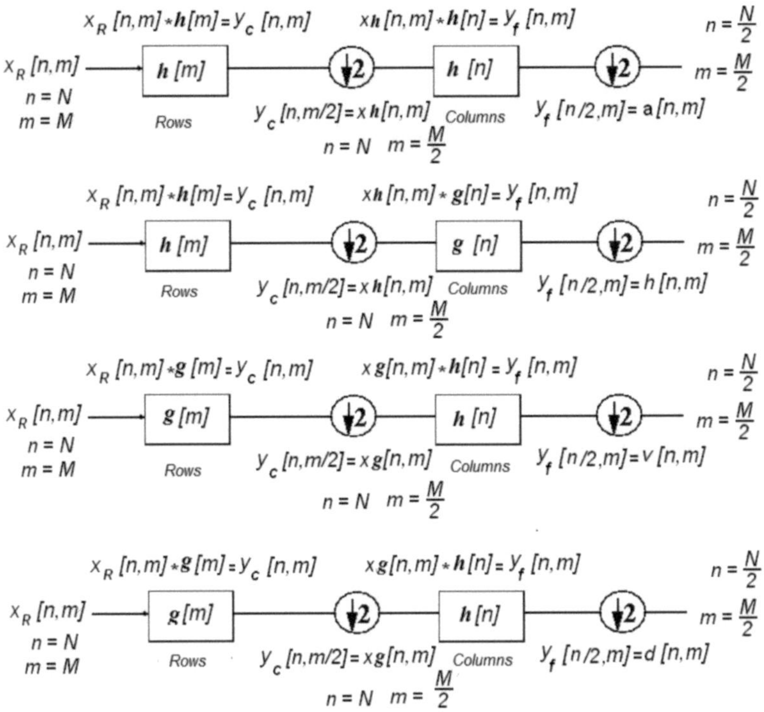

Fig. 4. Filter banks for encoding sub-bands representing the discrete wavelet decomposition of an image.

The discrete wavelet reconstruction can be computed by an inverse of the procedure of decomposition beginning for the level of resolution lower in the hierarchy and working from right hand to left side with the diagram of the Figure 4. The most of applications of steganographic algorithms are given in grayscale images, and the energy conservation in the wavelet domain is related to the factor $1/\sqrt{2}$ (Bogges A. et al. 2001; Walker J., 2003). In applying the proposed steganographic algorithm to the sub-matrix **h** is necessary to use a scaling factor that works with a 24-bit RGB color images; this scaling factor is closely related to energy conservation applied in the theory of wavelets. However, in the RGB color images we propose the following scaling factor,

$$1/\sqrt{2^n} \ , \tag{6}$$

where n is directly dependent on the number of bits that integrate the image.

3. Experimental results

In the optimization and evaluation of algorithms in digital image processing, the peak signal to noise relation (PSNR) is the criterion most frequently used to evaluate the quality of images (Huanga K. et al. 2005). However, the use of image qualitative measures is based on the properties of HVS, the models usually are embedded into HVS sensitivity to light and spatial frequency (Ginesu G. et al. 2006). Many measures used in the images during the visual information processing belong to the group of measures of difference in distortion (Kutter M. et al. 1999), is base on the difference between the original and modified images. The most common distortion measure is the PSNR defined as,

$$\mathrm{PSNR} = 10\ \log\left[\frac{(255)^2}{\mathrm{MSE}}\right]\ ,\mathrm{dB} \tag{7}$$

where $MSE = \frac{1}{M_1 M_2 M_3}\sum_{k=1}^{M_1}\sum_{i=1}^{M_2}\sum_{j=1}^{M_3}\left\| y(k,i,j) - x(k,i,j)\right\|_{L_2}^2$ is the Mean Square Error, M_1, M_2 and M_3 are the image dimensions, $y(k,i,j)$ is the 3D vector value of the pixel in the (k,i,j) location of the stego-image, $x(k,i,j)$ is the corresponding pixel in the original host image, and $\left\| \cdot \right\|_{L_2}$ is the L_2-vector norm. The Normalized Color Deviation (NCD) is used for the quantification of the color perceptual error,

$$\mathrm{NCD} = \frac{\sum_{i=1}^{M_1}\sum_{j=1}^{M_2}\left\|\Delta E_{Luv}(i,j)\right\|_{L_2}}{\sum_{i=1}^{M_1}\sum_{j=1}^{M_2}\left\|E_{Luv}^{*}(i,j)\right\|_{L_2}} \tag{8}$$

Here, $\left\|\Delta E_{Luv}(i,j)\right\|_{L_2} = \left[\left(\Delta L^{*}(i,j)\right)^2 + \left(\Delta u^{*}\right)^2 + \left(\Delta v^{*}\right)^2\right]^{1/2}$ is the norm of color error; ΔL^{*}, Δu^{*}, and Δv^{*} are the difference in the L^{*}, u^{*}, and v^{*} components, between the two color vectors that present the stego and host images for each pixel *(i,j)* of an image, and $\left\|E_{Luv}^{*}(i,j)\right\|_{L_2} = \left[\left(L^{*}\right)^2 + \left(u^{*}\right)^2 + \left(v^{*}\right)^2\right]^{1/2}$ is the norm of the host image pixel vector in the $L^{*}u^{*}v^{*}$ space.

The quality index (Q) is provided to demonstrate the quality of the stego-images (Wang Z. et al. 2002),

$$\mathrm{Q} = \frac{4\sigma_{xy}\overline{x}\overline{y}}{\left(\sigma_x^2 + \sigma_y^2\right)\left(\overline{x}^2 + \overline{y}^2\right)}\ , \tag{9}$$

where $\overline{x}$ and $\overline{y}$ are the mean values of the host and stego- images respectively, σ_x^2 and σ_y^2 are the variances of the host and stego-images respectively, and $\sigma_{xy} = \frac{1}{N\ \ 1}\sum_{i}^{N}(x_i\ \ \overline{x})(y_i\ \ \overline{y})$ is the coefficient correlation between host image *x* and hide image *y*.

The Hiding capacity (HC) is computed as follows (Sos S. et al. 2005),

$$HC = MSE * \frac{number\ of\ samples\ in\ embedding\ band}{number\ of\ bits\ of\ secure\ data} \tag{10}$$

where *HC* dictates that the number of bits inserted in the host image. Experimental results were conducted with 24-bit RGB images to show our mentioned scaling factor. As mentioned previously, the filtering can distort the images, as will be shown in subsequent tests applied filters to distort the host image with the DWT. An improvement in visual images can be perceived using the proposed scaling scheme. Additionally, We incorporate in the proposed scheme other color spaces such as YCbCr (Luminance, Chromatic blue, Chromatic red), and HSV (Hue, Saturation, Value) to ensure that the visual artifacts appeared in the stego-image are imperceptible, and the difference between the cover and stego image is indistinguishable by the HVS by using the proposed scaling factor.

Table 1 shows the performance results in terms of PSNR, MAE (Mean Absolute Error), COI (Correlation), Q, NCD, HC, and RMS (Root Mean Square) in the case of different *n* values in the scaling factor by using the 320 x 320 RGB color images "Mandrill" as host image and "Lena" as hide image. From Table 1, we can see that the *n* value increases, the performance results increase too, but the HC decreases because the hide image is inserted in each value of *n* in areas that do not affect the clarity of host image. Figure 5 depicts the processed images for stego-image Mandrill (Fig. 5a), 5b), and 5c)) and retrieved secret image Lena (Fig. 5d), 5e), and 5f)) according with Table 1. We observe from this Figure that the best results are obtained when *n*=9, where *n* represents the bits resolution of the image to hide. From Figs. 5d), 5e), and 5f) one can see that when the value of proposed scaling factor increases as well as the subjective quality of images increases too.

Tables 2 and 3 present the simulation results of the same test of Table 1 in the case of use of YCbCr and HSV color images (USC Vitterbi, 2011).

n		PSNR (dB)	COI %	NCD	Q	MAE	HC	RMS
n=0	Host image	31.5084	0.7852	0.0020	0.7836	10.4878	73.06Kb	0.4760
	Hide image	16.5327	0.388	0.4748	0.3586	4.9403		
n=2	Host image	31.4999	0.8046	0.0020	0.8040	9.9490	66.31Kb	0.4748
	Hide image	16.9537	0.3889	0.4749	0.3587	4.9471		
n=5	Host image	36.1233	0.9781	0.0020	0.9792	3.2086	61.97Kb	0.4614
	Hide image	27.2474	0.9985	0.0020	0.9962	2.7714		
n=9	Host image	36.1233	0.9908	0.0008	0.9913	2.0309	3.835Kb	0.4610
	Hide image	31.0781	0.9980	0.0020	0.9962	2.7714		

Table 1. Performance results for different *n* values for RGB color model.

n		PSNR (dB)	COI %	NCD	Q	MAE	HC	RMS
n=0	Host image	19.5146	0.8713	0.0020	0.8751	7.1762	26.34Kb	0.3961
	Hide image	2.7975	0.2008	0.0020	0.0601	178.1406		
n=2	Host image	19.7324	0.8782	0.0020	0.8816	7.0325	24.66Kb	0.4694
	Hide image	36.0827	0.9954	0.0020	0.9962	2.7948		
n=5	Host image	22.1046	0.9318	0.0015	0.9323	5.5328	12.30Kb	0.4202
	Hide image	36.0827	0.9954	0.0020	0.9962	2.7948		
n=9	Host image	28.5553	0.9836	0.0015	0.9843	2.7372	3.339Kb	0.4132
	Hide image	36.0827	0.9954	0.0020	0.9962	2.7948		

Table 2. Performance results for different *n* values for YCbCr color model.

n		PSNR (dB)	COI %	NCD	Q	MAE	HC	RMS
n=0	Host image	6.2955	0.5217	0.0020	0.0863	113.9768	0.359Kb	0.0020
	Hide image	2.8061	0.0592	0.0020	0.0003	177.9792		
n=2	Host image	20.1709	0.9015	0.0019	0.9067	5.6167	0.257Kb	0.0017
	Hide image	36.1233	0.9955	0.0020	0.9962	2.7714		
n=5	Host image	23.5030	0.9441	0.0010	0.9469	3.4113	0.568Kb	0.0013
	Hide image	36.1233	0.9955	0.0020	0.9962	2.7714		
n=9	Host image	38.8068	0.9985	0.0005	0.9985	0.8092	0.0713Kb	0.0012
	Hide image	36.1233	0.9955	0.0020	0.9962	2.7714		

Table 3. Performance results for different n values for HSV color model.

From the simulation results of Tables 1, 2, and 3 we can conclude that as the factor of scale is increasing we see in the results a visual improvement given for Q, COI, PSNR, RMS, etc; but according to this factor of scale is on the increase, a decrease exists in the capacity of insertion, is possible to see that the color model with major sacrifice in capacity of insertion is the HSV that offers the best visual results.

Table 4, shows the performance results in the n=10 case in the scaling factor. Figure 6 presents the visual results according with Table 4. We also present the error images. The proposed scaling factor $1/\sqrt{2^n}$ for each test presents a different result as can be seen in the previous tests, the scaling factor does not affect the steganographic algorithm preserving the energy of images. It can be seen that in the Lena error image of the Figure 6d), the difference value between the host image and the recovered image is approximately zero providing that the hidden information is almost imperceptible.

Fig. 5. Visual results for different n values in the scaling factor, a) and d) with n=2, b) and e) with n=5, and c) and f) n=9.

RGB color model	
Host image "Mandrill"	Hide image "Lena"
Q=0.9934	Q=0.9962
PSNR=36.1233 dB	PSNR=32.5167 dB
COI=99.34%	COI=99.55%
NCD=6.0486 e-4	NCD=0.0020
MAE=1.7022	MAE=2.7714
HC=25.65 kB	--------
YCbCr color model	
Host image "Mandrill"	Hide image "Lena"
Q=0.9888	Q=0.9962
PSNR=30.3913dB	PSNR=36.0827 dB
COI=98.92%	COI=99.54%
NCD=9.5940 e-4	NCD=0.0020
MAE=2.2044	MAE=2.7948
HC=2.18Kb	--------
HSV color model	
Host image "Mandrill"	Hide image "Lena"
Q=0.9993	Q=0.9962
PSNR=41.3900 dB	PSNR=36.1233 dB
COI=99.92%	COI=99.55%
NCD=2.8906 e-4	NCD=0.0020
MAE=0.6401	MAE=2.7714
HC=0.068Kb	--------

Table 4. Performance results in different color models for n=10 in the scaling factor.

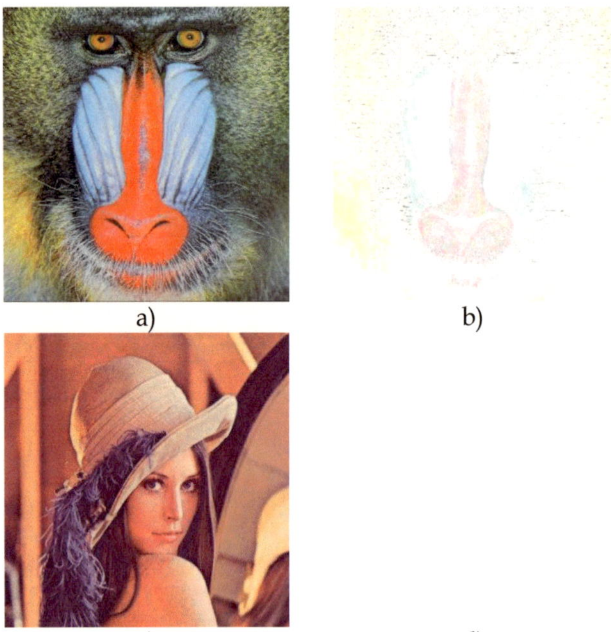

a) b)

c) d)

Fig. 6. Visual results in the case of n=10, a) stego-image "Mandrill, b) error stego-image "Mandrill, c) hide image "Lena", d) error hide image "Lena".

Finally, depending on the amount of information than we want to hide we can choose the model that best to hide information if that this one deform visibly the host image, in Table 4 we can see than the model of color HSV offers better quality in the stego-image in contrast to the RGB and YCbCr models, nevertheless capacity of insertion gets lost. It is possible to observe that the model RGB offers good results and capacity of insertion does not sacrifice itself.

4. Conclusions

The RGB, HSV and YCbCr color model images are altered in their energy contribution in each sub-matrix of wavelet decomposition when the steganographic algorithm is applied. It is known that the value of $1/\sqrt{2}$ is the key factor in the adjustment of the wavelets energy, this adjustment value has been applied only in gray scale images tests. However, the energy conservation factor mentioned above is not valid for true color images, such as formed by 3 submatrices (RGB, HSV and YCbCr) which separately provides some level of energy, that in sum contributes the quantity of entire energy, because if it is not right or there are energy gap in the components, the images may have a poor display as distortion. By applying the proposed scaling factor $1/\sqrt{2^n}$, there is an adjustment factor for the energy input in each submatrix. It is also noted that when is changing the value of n, it adjusts the sharpness and image clarity providing a visible improvement of the visual image. We conclude that the HSV model is suitable for small images. And for larger images it is advisable to use RGB model. The YCbCr model is the least suitable for steganography.

5. Acknowledgments

This work is supported by National Polytechnic Institute of Mexico and Conacyt.

6. References

Bogges Albert, Narcovich Francis, "A first course in wavelets with Fourier Analysis". Second edition. Ed. Wiley. ISBN:978-0-470-43117-7.

Carvajal-Gámez, B. E., Acevedo M., López-Bonilla, J.: Energy conservation in the concealment of information in a video by means of discrete wavelet transform. IeJEMTA 4, 27-31 (2008)

Carvajal-Gámez, B.E.: "Técnica de Inserción de Información en Video aprovechando el mismo Ancho de Banda", Master Disertation Thesis, ESIME-Zacatenco, National Polythecnic Institute (2008)

Chia-Chen, L., Wei-Liang, T., Chin-Chen C.: Multilevel reversible data hiding based on histogram modification of difference. Pattern Recognition. 3582-3591 (2008)

Chung-Ming, W., Nan-I W., Chwei-Shyong, T., Min-Shiang H.: A high quality steganographic method with pixel value differencing and modulus function. Journal of System and Software. 150-158 (2008)

Data Base Images of the University of Southern of California, (2011), Signal and Image Processing Institute. USC VITERBI. http://sipi.usc.edu/database/database.php.(2011)

Debnath, L.: Wavelets and Signal Processing, (2002),Birkhauser, ISBN: 0-8176-4235-8, Berlin.

Ginesu, G., Massidda, F., Giusto, D.D.: A multi-factors approach for image quality assessment based on a human visual system model. Signal Processing: Image communication. 316-333 (2006)

Huanga, K.Q., Wub, Z.Y., Fungc, G.S.K., Chan, H.Y.: Color image denoising with wavelet thresholding based on human visual system model. Signal Processing: Image communication. 115-127 (2005)

Kutter, M., Petitcolas, F.A.P.: A fair benchmark for image watermarking systems. Proc. SPIE Electronic Imaging '99. Security and Watermarking of Multimedia Contents. 1-14 (1999)

Martin Vetterli, Jelena Kovacevic and Vivek K Goyal: Fourier and wavelet signal processing,(2011), Alpha version book 2.0. http://fourierandwavelets.org.(2011)

Moon, H.S., You, T., Sohn, M.H., Kim, H.S., Jang, D.S.: Expert system for low frequency adaptive image watermarking: Using psychological experiments on human image perception. Expert Systems with Applications. 674-686 (2007)

Petrosian, A.A., Meyers, F.G.: Wavelets in Signal and Image Analysis, (2002), Kluwer Academic Pub., ISBN:978-1- 4020-0053-9, Berlin.

Reddy, A.A., Chatterji, B.N.: A new wavelet based logo-watermarking scheme. Pattern Recognition Lett. 1019-1027 (2005)

Sos S. Agaian, David Akopian and Sunil A. D'Souza "Frequency Domain Based Secure Digital Audio Steganography Algorithms," IEEE SP/CAS, 2005 International Workshop on Spectral Methods and Multirate Signal Processing, SMMS, June 20-22, 2005, Riga, Latvia.

Vetterli, M., Kočević, J.: Wavelets and Subband Coding, (1995), Prentice-Hall, ISBN:978-0130970800 New Jersey

Walker, J.: A primer on wavelets and their scientific applications, (2003), Chapman & Hall/CRC, ISBN: 1584887451, London.

Wang - Zhou, Bovik C. Alan.: A universal quality index. IEEE Signal Processing Letters.81-84 (2002)

Y. Sheng, "The Transforms and Applications Handbook". Ed. 2nd, CRC Press, (2000), ISBN: 9780849385957 .

Yuan-Hui,Y., Chin-Chen, C.,Yu-Chen, H.: Hiding secret data in images via predictive coding. Pattern Recognition. 691-705 (2005)

3

RABS: Rule-Based Adaptive Batch Steganography

Hedieh Sajedi
Department of Computer Science, Tehran University, Iran

1. Introduction

Steganography is used mostly when the fact of communicating needs to be kept covert. This is carried out by embedding the secret data in apparently innocuous covers. Typical covers are image, video, and audio files (Munuera, 2007). For steganographic systems, the major requirement is that the stego object should be perceptually and statistically indistinguishable to the degree that it does not raise suspicion. In other words, the hidden information should impose slight or undetectable modification to the cover objects (Wu & Shih, 2006).

The steganography methods that embed secret data in Discrete Cosine Transform (DCT) of images are well known because of the vast usage of JPEG images. Steganography methods like F5 (Westfeld,2001), Model-based (MB) (Sallee, 2003), Perturbed Quantization (PQ) (Fridrich et al. 2004), and YASS (Solanki et al. 2007) manipulate some DCT coefficients for embedding the secret data. Some other methods have been proposed which embed secret information in other transform domains, such as Contourlet-based steganography method (Sajedi & Jamzad, 2008) that hides secret data in contourlet coefficients of a cover image.

Stego version of images may have different grades of visual and statistical undetectability due to their different contents. It is shown in (Wu & Shih, 2006) that, when the size of hidden data gets larger than a threshold then it becomes easier for a steganalysis algorithm to detect the presence of the hidden data. Consequently, a steganography method can employ a technique to embed in a cover image until it does not attract the attention of steganalysis methods and makes steganalyzers to misclassify the observed stego image as a cover (clean) image. In this way, we can find an upper bound for embedding rate such that if the size of hidden data is less than that upper bound, the stego image is safe and it can not be detected by steganalysis methods.

So far, the performance of a steganography method is evaluated in its average steganography capacity. However, there is no guarantee that a specific stego image could not be detected reliably by the steganalyzers. In this chapter, we propose an approach to estimate the steganography capacity of images. Then, the steganographer can embed securely a secret data with the size smaller than or equal to the steganography capacity of the image.

In investigating the problem from a theoretical model, in order to obtain the actual results, the statistical models of images should be simplified to an extent that would cause the results less relevant. Instead of using statistical models, we extract the signature of cover images as a practical model for images and evaluate the security of stego images with respect to this model.

The usual concept of steganography assumes that the steganographer embeds the secret data in only one cover image and passes it on to the recipient by means of a communication channel. Since the steganography capacity of an image is limited (Fridrich et al. ,2007), to hide a large secret data securely, we have to split the secret data to some parts and embed each part in a cover image. Consequently, the large secret data is hidden in a set of cover images and the resulted set of stego images is passed through the communication channel. This technique is called Batch steganography, which is first proposed by Ker (Ker, 2006). He states in (Ker, 2008) that in batch steganography, the best choice for the steganographer is to spread the secret data equally between cover images. This statement is due to the assumptions considered to simplify the theoretical presentation of batch steganography.

In (Sajedi& Jamzad, 2009) to describe the problem in batch steganography, we called the Ker's definition of batch steganography as Static Batch Steganography (SBS). SBS divides the secret data into some parts of equal size and embeds each part in a cover image separately (Ker, 2006; Ker, 2008). Since in SBS the steganographer embeds in cover images blindly without considering the differences between various cover images, two problems may be occurred. First, the steganographer may embed in an image less than its steganography capacity. In this case, the steganographer has not used the steganography capacity of the image efficiently. The second problem occurs when the steganographer hides secret data in an image while the size of secret data is larger than the steganography capacity of image. Consequently, the security of the resulted stego image is reduced. In fact, SBS assumes identical steganography capacity for each cover image independent of its content. In SBS, a small part of secret data is embedded in each image so as the security of the produced stego image is not threatened.

Previously, we proposed an adaptive batch steganography called ABS in (Sajedi& Jamzad, 2009). In this method, an ensemble of steganalyzers determines the steganography capacity of images and then the secret data is divided based on the steganography capacity of cover images. In (Sajedi& Jamzad, 2009), the estimation time of steganography capacity is rather high because the feature extraction part of steganalyzers, which are used in the ensemble steganalyzer, is done completely. As we know, the feature extraction part of each steganalyzer is the most time-consuming part of it. Consequently, in this chapter we tend to reduce the estimation time of steganography capacity in adaptive batch steganography.

We propose Rule-based Adaptive Batch Steganography (RABS) in which we estimate the steganography capacity of each image according to the signature of clean images. Therefore, instead of embedding a constant amount of data in each image as Ker proposed, we embed unequal amounts of secret data in each image reliant to its steganography capacity. RABS is an intelligent solution to the problem of hiding a large secret data and it guaranties the security of stego images against the existing steganalyzers.

On the other hand, since the communication channel is limited, we prefer to have the lowest number of images in the stego image set to occupy the communication channel lesser. RABS attempts to decrease the number of required cover images by applying an intelligent cover selection approach. In this approach, to hide a large secret data we split the payload and embed each part in an image with steganography capacity of equal or higher than the secret data part.

Generally, in batch steganography by considering the steganography capacity of images, the steganographer can embed securely every large-size secret data in a set of images, which are selected to have a sufficient total steganography capacity. In RABS, for embedding a secret data with a certain size, the database is checked and a set of proper cover images is suggested for embedding. This strategy can be used with any existing steganography methods.

In this chapter, steganography capacity of images is estimated by extracting and using the signature of clean images. Our approach first analyzes an image database to discover the signature of clean images. By the signature, we mean the effective features of clean images and their relative values. This signature is a set of fuzzy if-then rules that represents similarity between clean images. A secure stego image is the one that after data hiding stimulates the generated fuzzy rules significantly and follows the signature of clean images. The process of generating the signature of clean images is done by an Evolutionary Algorithm (EA). EA have been used as rule induction and optimization tools in design of fuzzy rule-based systems (Cordon et al. 2009, Hu et al. 2003).

We considered steganography capacity measure in applying MB, PQ, and YASS steganography techniques and validated it using an image database. The results illustrate that embedding in cover images based on their steganography capacity reduces the detection accuracy of state-of-the-art steganalysis methods considerably compared to the traditional usage of the steganography methods. In addition, we used RABS for hiding some large secret data in cover image sets and compared the results with ABS and SBS.

The rest of this chapter is organized as follows. In Section 2, we describe the related works. RABS method is presented in Section 3. Steganography capacity estimation based on signature of clean images is described in Section 4. We explain the experimental results in Section 5. Finally, we conclude our work in Section 6.

2. Related works

2.1 Batch steganography

Batch steganography is hiding the secret data into multiple cover objects. It seems that considering a fixed secret data length, the embedding in many cover objects will reduce the embedding rate for each image and thus make the detection harder. Moreover, a recent paper by Fridrich (Fridrich et al. ,2007) highlights the fact that whatever the steganography algorithm, it remains highly detectable when the embedding rate is above a threshold (0.05 bits per non-zero DCT coefficients). The use of small embedding rates provided by batch steganography seems attractive in this sense. Ker in (Ker, 2006) takes the main following assumptions about the batch steganography process:

- The number of cover objects is fixed.
- All cover objects have the same steganography capacity.
- The data to embed is of fixed length.
- The number of cover objects is known to the steganalyzer.

Additionally, Ker in (Ker, 2008) states that the best choice of the steganographer is to spread payload equally between covers. As discussed in (Ker, 2006), some of these assumptions are taken in order to establish a proper theoretical framework for the unexplored subject of batch steganography. However, these assumptions may not be totally applicable to a practical case. For example, if the number of cover images is low and the total capacity of cover images is not enough to conceal the secret data, then each resulted stego image is overloaded, and its security would be low. If the number of cover images is high, with spreading the secret data equally between cover images, then the security of stego images is high but the communication channel will be occupied a lot.

2.2 Steganography capacity

A number of ways to compute the steganography capacity have been proposed previously (Chandramouli, & Memon , 2003- Sajedi & Jamzad,2009a). A definition of steganography capacity is presented in (Chandramouli & Memon,2003) from a steganalysis perspective. This work argues that as the main goal of steganography is hidden communications, steganography capacity is dependent on the type of steganalysis detector employed to break the embedding algorithm. It defines γ-security so that in presence of a steganalysis detector D, a steganography algorithm is said to be perfectly secure if $\gamma D = 0$.

The work in (Cachin, 1998) defines a steganography method to be ε-secure ($\varepsilon \geq 0$) if the relative entropy between the cover and the stego probability distributions (Pc and Ps, respectively) is at most ε, i.e.,

$$D(P_c|P_s) = \int P_c \log \frac{P_c}{P_s} \leq \varepsilon \quad (1)$$

A stego technique is said to be perfectly secure if $\varepsilon = 0$. This definition assumes that the cover and stego images are independent identically distributed (i.i.d.) random variables. This assumption is not true for many real life cover signals (Chandramouli & Memon,2003). One approach to rectify this is to put the constraint that the relative entropy computed using the nth order joint probability distributions must be less than εn. One can then force a steganography technique to preserve the n order distribution. But, it may then be possible to use (n+1) order statistics for steganalysis. The research in (Moulin & Mihcak, 2002) provides an estimate of steganography capacity of images, based on a parallel Gaussian model.

Ker in (Ker, 2007) defines batch steganography capacity and theoretically proves that the size of secret data can safely increase no faster than square root of the number of cover images.

In (Sajedi & Jamzad,2009a), an ensemble system that uses different steganalyzer units, considers the steganography capacity by determining the security limits for embedding in cover images. In this system, each steganalyzer unit is formed by a combination of multiple steganalyzers from the same type. Each steganalyzer in a steganalyzer unit is trained to detect stego images with a certain payload. The upper bound of embedding rate for an image is determined based on the confidence of all the steganalyzers about the image. In fact, considering steganography capacity, the steganographer can minimize the risk of detection by selecting from a database a proper cover image that is secure for a certain payload. To calculate the steganography capacity of an image, the embedding rate is increased steadily until the security of the produced stego image is threatened by the ensemble steganalyzer. The time (t) required for secure embedding (Sajedi & Jamzad,2009a) is shown by equation (2):

$$t = t_s + t_{sce}$$

$$t_{sce} = k \times (t_s + \sum_{i=1}^{I} t_{su}(i)) \; ; \; t_{su}(i) = \sum_{j=1}^{k} t_{sz}^{i}(j) \tag{2}$$

where t_{sce} is the time of steganography capacity estimation, t_s is the embedding time of employed steganography method, k is the number of iterations of incremental embedding algorithm and $t_{su}(i)$ is the time of the ith steganalyzer unit. I is the number of steganalysis units that are used in the ensemble steganalyzer and $t_{sz}^{i}(j)$ is the time required for the jth steganalyzer that is trained for detection of stego images with payload of multiple j in the ith steganalyzer unit. Although the time complexity of secure embedding (Sajedi & Jamzad,2009a) is more than traditional embedding, but since it provides more secure stego images, its time complexity can be acceptable. Due to differences in contents of various images, the total time of incremental embedding may differ. Considering the fact that the main goal of steganography is to embed the secret data securely and if any of the steganalyzers gets suspicious, then the purpose of steganography is broken, therefore it is worth to spend further time to make stego images more secure.

In this chapter, the evolutionary rule induction algorithm, which is proposed in (Sajedi & Jamzad,2009b) is employed. The generated fuzzy rule base is used to form the signature of clean images and afterward to estimate the steganography capacity of images.

2.3 RABS: Rule-based Adaptive Batch Steganography

Considering steganography capacity of an image, we can embed in the image a portion of secret data that its size is less or equal to the steganography capacity of the image. The remaining unconcealed portion of secret data can be hidden in some other cover images. Our approach aims to improve the undetectability of stego images while utilizing the cover images perfectly. Additionally, RABS tries to hide a large secret data in a cover image set very quickly. Differing from the static batch steganography (Cachin, 1998; Cordon et al. 2009), a more practical approach is used in this chapter which its details and procedure is described in the following. Our assumptions are as follows:

1. The steganographer has the option to select cover images from an image database.
2. The size of secret data can be variable.
3. The number of cover images in a cover image set can be variable.

4. The receiver knows the strategy of steganographer for breaking the payload into some parts and the order of stego images.

The steganographer can select cover images randomly from the database or based on their steganography capacities to minimize the detection rate and the number of images in the stego image set. In RABS, at first the steganography capacity of cover images is estimated using 'Signature of Clean Images' (which is described in the next section) and then the embedding algorithm is activated.

The following steps demonstrate the embedding algorithm of RABS approach. Let CI denotes the steganography capacity of image I and EDS denotes the size of embedding secret data. The inputs of the algorithm are SDS, IDB, and CIS that respectively denotes secret data size, image database, and signature of clean images. The output of the algorithm is SIS, which denotes the stego image set.

Step 1. Select cover image I from IDB and set $EDS=0$.

Step 2. Hide portions of secret data incrementally until the image deviates from CIS. The size of data that is embedded in the image shows the steganography capacity C_I of image I. Set $EDS = EDS + C_I$.

Step 3. Add the stego image to SIS.

If $SDS > EDS$ then

Select a new cover image from IDB to embed the remaining part of the secret data. Go to step 2.

Otherwise,

SIS is the output.

Figure 1 shows the block diagram of steganography capacity estimation. In RABS, embedding is continuing in different cover images until the secret data become concealed completely. Steganographer can select cover images in random or based on a cover selection criterion. To reduce the number of images in stego image set, the steganographer can employ a cover selection strategy and choose cover images with higher steganography capacities. The image that is the output of the incremental embedding routine is a secure stego image because it conceals a part of secret data that its size is not more than the steganography capacity of the image.

3. Steganography capacity estimation

3.1 Signature extraction of clean images

In this chapter, we utilize an iterative evolutionary fuzzy algorithm for estimation of steganography capacity of images. In this utilization, the algorithm extracts a fuzzy rule base for obtaining the signature of clean images. Consequently, to have a secure covert communication, we can embed in an image until it deviates from the clean images signature. It should be noted that the embedding procedure could be carried on by any steganography method.

It is generally believed that a blind steganalyzer trained on sufficiently many diverse steganography algorithms will become universal in the sense that it will generalize to previously unseen (novel) steganography methods. While this is a partially correct statement if the embedding mechanism of the novel method resembles some of the methods on which the classifier was trained (Pevny & Fridrich, 2008), it demonstrated that if the classifier is presented with stego images produced by a completely different embedding mechanism, it may fail to detect the images as stego even for an easily detectable method. Motivated by this observation, (Pevny & Fridrich, 2008) explored two approaches for construction of universal steganalyzers—one-class and one-against-all classifiers. One-against-all classifiers may fail on previously unseen stego algorithms. One-class methods are less likely to fail to detect unknown stego algorithms. Considering the above discussion, to have more generalization capability and to cover unseen steganography methods, we model clean images instead of stego images according to the method shown in Figure 1.

The process of extracting steganographic features from an image is a mapping $f: C \mapsto \mathbb{R}^d$ from the space of all the covers, C, to a d-dimensional feature space. In steganalysis, learning methods are used to find a distinguishing statistics $S: \mathbb{R}^d \mapsto \mathbb{R}$, on which a threshold is set to classify images to the classes of cover and stego (Pevny et al., 2009).

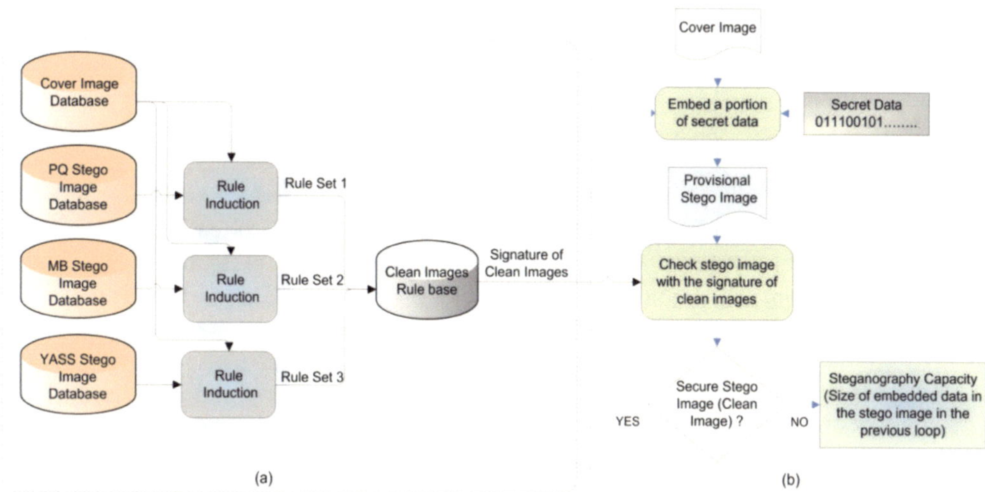

Fig. 1. The block diagram of steganography capacity estimation, (a) Extracting signature of clean images by evolutionary fuzzy rule induction, (b) Steganography capacity estimation by incremental embedding.

In our current problem we seek a function $\varphi: \mathbb{R}^d \mapsto R^{n1}$ revealing the signature of clean images (i.e. significant features with their values for cover images), where R demonstrates fuzzy rules and $n \ll d$.

The signature of clean images $CIS = \left\{ R_j = \{(x_i, y_i) | x_i \in \mathbb{R}^d, y_i \in L^n, i \in \{1,...,l\}\} \middle| j \in \{1,...,J\} \right\}$ is a set of j fuzzy rules with length of i and L includes linguistic fuzzy values. Following subsections describe the details of this approach.

3.2 Feature extraction

We use the feature vector $X = \left\{ x_i \middle| x_i \in \mathbb{R}^d, i \in \{1,...,d\} \right\}$, which is produced by appending the features of four efficient and well-known steganalyzers. 636 features are computed according to the features of Pevny-Fridrich (Pevný & Fridrich, 2007), Chen et. al (Chen et. al, 2006), Lyu-Farid (Lyu & Farid, 2002), and Li et. al (Li et. Al, 2008) steganalysis methods. In the following, we briefly review the features used by these steganalyzers.

1. Pevny and Fridrich (Pevný & Fridrich, 2007) extract 274 features by merging 193 extended DCT features with 81 averaged calibrated Markov features. However, many of the 274 features may be highly correlated to each other. In this method, Markov features model intra block DCT dependencies and DCT features model inter block relations. In the rest of this chapter, we refer to this steganalysis method as 274-dim steganalyzer.
2. In (Chen et. al, 2006), Chen et. al proposed a steganalysis method that employs a 324-dimensional feature vector for analysis. It is based on statistical moments derived from both image 2-D array and JPEG 2-D array. This steganalyzer considers both the first order and the second order histograms. Consequently, the moments of 2-D characteristic functions are also used for steganalysis. In the following, this method is referred to as 324-dim steganalyzer.
3. Wavelet-based steganalysis method (Lyu & Farid, 2002), presented by Lyu and Farid, builds a model for clean images by using higher order statistics, and then shows the deviation of stego images from the constructed model. Quadratic Mirror Filters are used to decompose the image into wavelet domain, after which higher order statistics such as mean, variance, skewness, and kurtosis are calculated for each subband. The higher order statistics are calculated from wavelet coefficients of each high-frequency subband to form one group of features. Another group of features is similarly formulated from the prediction errors of wavelet coefficients of each high-frequency subband. We called this method WBS steganalyzer.
4. Yet Another Steganographic Scheme (YASS) (Solanki et al. 2007) is designed to be a secure JPEG steganographic algorithm. Attacking YASS is proposed in Li et. al (Li et. Al, 2008). The success of YASS is attributed to its innovation in embedding, i.e., hiding data in embedding cover blocks whose locations are randomized. However, the locations of the embedding host blocks are not randomized enough. Some locations in an image are possible to hold an entire embedding cover block and some locations are definitely not. Additionally, YASS employs a Quantization Index Modulation embedding strategy in order to enhance the robustness of the embedded data, which on the other hand introduces extra zero coefficients into the embedding cover blocks during data hiding. Consequently, statistical features extracted from locations, which are possible to hold embedding cover blocks are different from those locations, which are impossible to hold embedding cover blocks. Here we called this method YASS-steganalyzer.

Table 1 depicts the types of all the 636 features.

Feature Group	Number of Features	Feature Type
274	11	Global Histogram
	66	5 AC Histograms
	99	11 Dual Histograms
	1	Variation
	2	Blockiness
	25	Co-occurrence Matrix
	81	Markov Features
324	39	Histogram of Spatial Representation and Discrete Wavelet Transform (DWT) Representation.
	39	Histogram of Prediction Error and DWT of Error
	39	Histogram of JPEG Representation and its DWT.
	78	Horizontal 2-D Histogram of JPEG Representation and its DWT 2-D Histogram
	78	Vertical 2-D Histogram of JPEG Representation and its DWT 2-D Histogram
	78	Diagonal 2-D Histogram of JPEG Representation and its DWT.
	39	Histogram obtained from Prediction Error of JPEG representation and its DWT
24	24	Higher order statistics of each Wavelet subband.
14	14	A group of frequencies of zero rounded re-quantized DCT coefficients.

Table 1. Types of 636 image features

3.3 Fuzzy rule induction

We code every fuzzy if-then rule as a string and use the following symbols for denoting the six linguistic values: 1: don't care (*DC*), 2: small (*S*), 3: medium small (*MS*), 4: medium (*M*), 5: medium large (*ML*), 6: large (*L*). The fuzzy rules are as follows:

$$\textit{Rule } R_j : \textit{If} \, (x_1 \text{ is } y_1 \text{ and} \ldots \text{and } x_n \text{ is } y_n) \; \textit{then} \text{ Image is clean with } CF = CF_j .$$

where R_j is the label of the jth fuzzy if-then rule, $\{x_i | x_i \in \mathbb{R}^d\}$ are the features extracted from the observed image, $\{y_i \mid y_i \in L^n\}$ are linguistic values that represent *S*, *MS*, *M*, *ML*, *L*, and *DC*. CF_j is the certainty grade of fuzzy if-then rule R_j. Each fuzzy rule has a certainty grade that demonstrates the confidence of the rule about its antecedent part.

The membership function of each linguistic value is specified by homogeneously partitioning the domain of each feature into symmetric triangular fuzzy sets. The total number of possible fuzzy if-then rules is 6^d (due to using six linguistic values) in case of d-dimensional feature vector. It is impossible to use all the 6^d fuzzy if-then rules in a single fuzzy rule base for large d (e.g. steganography capacity estimation based on d = 636 features). Therefore, the employed evolutionary method searches for a relatively small number of fuzzy if-then rules (e.g., J = 10 rules) with higher performance. By performance, we mean that the inducted fuzzy if-then rules should be able to show the pattern or signature of clean images with high accuracy. This signature is extracted according to the training samples of clean and stego images.

The outline of the employed evolutionary fuzzy method is presented in (Sajedi & Jamzad,2009b). We apply the following three steps to calculate the certainty grade of each fuzzy if-then rule:

Step 1: Calculate the compatibility of each training sample $X_p = (x_{p1}, x_{p2}, \ldots, x_{pn})$ with the fuzzy if-then rule R_j by the following product operation:

$$\mu_j(X_p) = \mu_{j1}(x_{p1}) \times \ldots \times \mu_{jl}(x_{pl}), \quad \begin{matrix} P = 1,2,\ldots,M \\ l \leq n \end{matrix} \tag{3}$$

where $\mu_{ji}(x_{pi})$ is the membership function of ith feature of pth sample and M denotes the total number of samples.

Step 2: For clean and stego images, calculate the relative sum of the compatibility grades of training samples with fuzzy if-then rule R_j :

$$\beta_{Clean}(R_j) = \frac{\sum_{X_p \in Clean} \mu_j(X_p)}{N_{Clean}} \tag{4}$$

$$\beta_{Stego}(R_j) = \frac{\sum_{X_p \in Stego} \mu_j(X_p)}{N_{Stego}} \tag{5}$$

where $\beta_{Clean}(R_j)$ and $\beta_{Stego}(R_j)$ are the relative sum of the compatibility grades of training samples that represent clean and stego images, respectively. Note that N_{Clean} and N_{Stego} represent the number of clean and stego images that are being used as training samples.

Step 3: The grade of certainty CF_j is determined as follows:

$$CF_j = \frac{\left(\beta_{Clean}(R_j) - \beta_{Stego}(R_j)\right)}{\left(\beta_{Clean}(R_j) + \beta_{Stego}(R_j)\right)} \tag{6}$$

The employed evolutionary fuzzy algorithm learns fuzzy if-then rules by optimizing one fuzzy rule in each iteration of the algorithm. At first, all the training samples have the same weight and each individual in the algorithm is initialized by the feature vector of an image. In each iteration of the algorithm, the rule with highest fitness is considered as the output of the iteration. Then the learning mechanism reduces the weight of those training samples that are learned correctly. Samples with higher weight are more significant in the training process. Therefore, the next rule induction cycle, searches for fuzzy rules that cover the training samples, which are uncovered by the rules obtained in previous iterations. In brief, the fuzzy rules that cover the training samples more than other rules are included in the final rule base.

Reducing the weight of training samples helps to aggregate different disciplines between features of training samples to form a perfect fuzzy rule base. In the above learning framework, we have used a fitness function in evolutionary process. It is computed according to equations (7) to (9).

$$f_P = \frac{\sum_{X_k \in Clean} w^k \mu_{R_j}(X_k)}{\sum_{X_k \in Clean} w^k} \tag{7}$$

$$f_N = \frac{\sum_{X_k \in Stego} w^k \mu_{R_j}(X_k)}{\sum_{X_k \in Stego} w^k} \tag{8}$$

$$fitness(R_j) = w_P \, f_P - w_N \, f_N \tag{9}$$

where, f_P is the rate of positive training samples covered by rule R_j (correctly covered), f_N is the rate of negative training samples covered by rule R_j (wrongly covered), w^k is a weight which reflects the frequency of the sample X_k in the training database, w_P is the weight of rule's positive power, and w_N is the weight of rule's negative power.

Each stego image database and clean image database are shown to the rule induction algorithm (we set the parameters of MB, PQ, and YASS to construct stego image databases with variety of payloads). Afterward, a clean image rule set is resulted considering the effects of a steganography method on images. We have three types of stego image databases (MB, PQ, and YASS), therefore, three sets of rules are inducted. Putting all the rules of clean images in a clean image rule base, we obtain the signature of clean images.

3.4 Determining steganography capacity of an image

To determine the steganography capacity of an image an incremental embedding routine is applied. It steadily increases embedding rate until the stego image does not move away from the signature of clean images. Figure 1(b) illustrates the block diagram of incremental embedding routine.

For a given rule base S, in order to determine steganography capacity of an image with feature vector $X_p = (x_{p1}, x_{p2}, \ldots, x_{pn})$ is reliable to host a secret data, two parameters τ_{Clean} and τ_{Stego} are computed using equations (10) and (11). After hiding the secret data in the cover image, τ_{Stego} is computed based on the features $X_{ps} = (x_{ps1}, x_{ps2}, \ldots, x_{psn})$ of the produced stego image.

$$\tau_{Clean} = \sum_{R_j \in S} \mu_j(X_p)\, CF_j \tag{10}$$

$$\tau_{Stego} = \sum_{R_j \in S} \mu_j(X_{ps})\, CF_j \tag{11}$$

Generally, equation (12) is valid for a pair of clean and stego images because the rule base S contains rules that are achieved from with regard to clean images. Consequently, a clean image is more compatible with these rules compared to its stego version. If τ, the difference of τ_{Clean} and τ_{Stego}, is lower than threshold T in equation (13), it means that the clean and stego images are not distinguishable and the security of the cover image is acceptable. Since we can say that a clean image is a stego image with hidden data size of zero, so for a cover image τ_{Clean} is equal to τ_{Stego}. While embedding in the image steadily and examining its features with the signature of clean images, τ_{Stego} decreases and so the value of τ increases little by little. Thus, for determining the steganography capacity of an images we embed in the image incrementally until $\tau < T$. Finally, the steganography capacity of the images is equal to the size of embedded data.

$$\tau_{Clean} \succ \tau_{Stego} \tag{12}$$

$$\tau = (\tau_{Clean} - \tau_{Stego}) \prec T \tag{13}$$

Considering capacity limit in steganography, the steganographer can embed in an image until the stego image is undetectable. To produce a secure stego image, the secret data is embedded in the image and the resulted stego image is evaluated according to the signature of clean images. If the stego image deviates from the signature significantly, the cover image is overloaded and the steganographer can reduce the payload.

4. Experiments

For signature extraction of clean images, we used Camera image database of Binghamton University (Cancelli et.al ,2008), which has 3164 grayscale images of size 512×512. To evaluate the performance of RABS approach, we obtained 1000 JPEG images from both Washington University image database (washington.edu) and Internet. All images are converted to grayscale and cropped to size of 512×512.

In this chapter, we measure the separation of feature vectors of cover and stego images by training a non-linear SVM classifier with RBF kernel and use the accuracy of steganalysis as a measure of detectability (Fridrich et.al ,2007). Detection accuracy being close to 50 implies nearly undetectable hiding, and as the detectability improves, detection accuracy increases towards 100. To make stego image databases, MB, PQ, and YASS steganography methods are employed. We set the parameters of these methods to different values to obtain three stego image databases with variety of payloads. Each stego database has 1000 stego images.

Our experiments were executed on a personal computer with a 2046 MB PIV processor using Matlab R2007.

In our implementation environment, the average time for incremental embedding in one image and determining the steganography capacity of the image is around 20 seconds. This time is around 2 minutes when the ABS is employed (Cordon et.al ,2004). As the result shows, RABS is less time-consuming than ABS. Therefore, using RABS a large secret data can be hidden in a cover image set more quickly compared to ABS. Since secure data embedding is the main goal of steganography and if any of the steganalyzers gets suspicious, the purpose of steganography is broken, it is worth to spend more time to make stego images more secure.

4.1 Performance of RABS

RABS can apply every existing steganography method. Table 2 shows the detection accuracy of four steganalyzers on the proposed RABS, ABS, and the traditional usage of PQ, MB, and YASS steganography methods. Employing WBS, 274-dim, 324-dim, and YASS steganalysis (denoted by YASS analyzer in the table) methods, to train the SVM classifier of each steganalyzer, 1200 (600 clean and 600 stego) images from the image database were used. The remaining 800 images are used for testing. As we see in Table 2, the results obviously show that the stego images, which are produced by RABS, are less detectable than the stego images constructed by traditional usage of steganography methods. In providing security for stego images, RABS approach operates close to ABS.

It should be noted that in ABS, the steganography capacity of an image is determined without considering the steganalysis method of YASS.

Figure 2 shows the average accuracy of steganalyzers in detection of stego images with different payloads produced by traditional usage of steganography methods, ABS, and RABS. In most of the cases, ABS' and RABS' undetectability are very close to each other. Both, ABS and RABS produce stego images with much higher security than traditional usage of steganography methods.

Steganography method	Average Payload (bits)	Steganalysis detection accuracy (%)											
		Traditional steganography method				ABS				RABS			
		WBS	274-dim	324-dim	YASS analyzer	WBS	274-dim	324-dim	YASS analyzer	WBS	274-dim	324-dim	YASS analyzer
PQ	2000	72	74	57	-	53	53	52	-	55	56	53	-
	6000	76	77	83	-	55	58	56	-	56	58	58	-
	10000	79	79	91	-	56	60	59	-	59	61	60	-
MB	2000	71	67	89	-	51	54	59	-	51	54	54	-
	6000	77	72	96	-	56	52	56	-	56	52	56	-
	10000	86	81	99	-	56	57	58	-	59	60	59	-
YASS	2000	55	57	59	72	52	56	57	72	52	55	55	56
	6000	62	63	57	86	56	58	57	86	59	59	57	61
	10000	61	69	65	97	59	60	59	97	59	60	59	65

Table 2. Accuracy of steganalysis methods in detection of stego images produced by different steganography methods (in percent

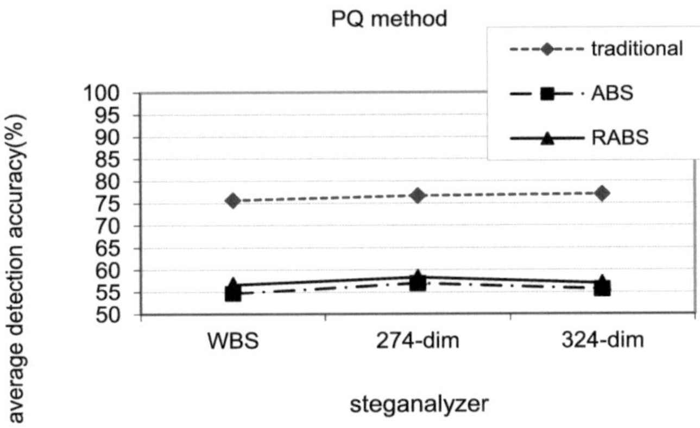

(a)

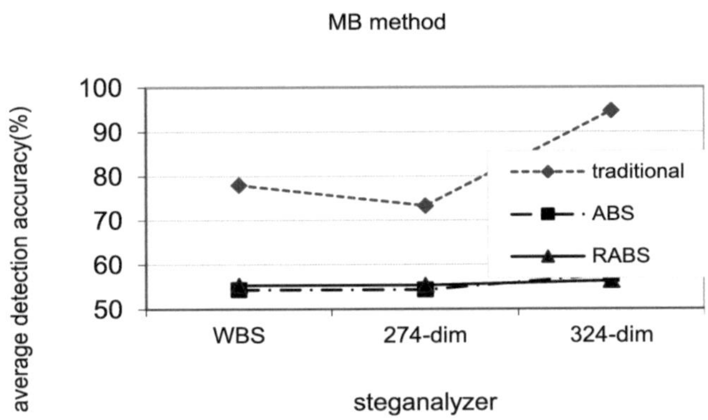

(b)

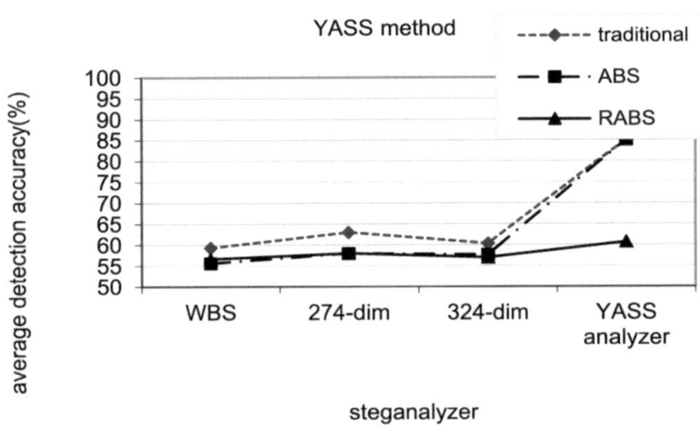

(c)

Fig. 2. Average detection accuracy of steganalysis methods on (a) PQ, (b) MB, and (c) YASS steganography methods.

Figure 4 shows the relationship between the number of members in a cover image set and the total steganography capacity of it. White columns are computed by square root law, as described by Ker et al. in (Ker, 2007). Light gray columns show the average capacity of the cover image sets when their members are selected randomly. Dark gray and black columns show the average capacity of the cover image sets when their members are selected using ABS and RABS respectively from images having top 40% higher capacity in the database. As the Figure 4 shows, random selection columns are close to the square root law columns. In square root law, we suppose that cover images have equal steganography capacities. However, selection of cover images based on steganography capacity (as suggested by ABS and RABS methods) breaks this law.

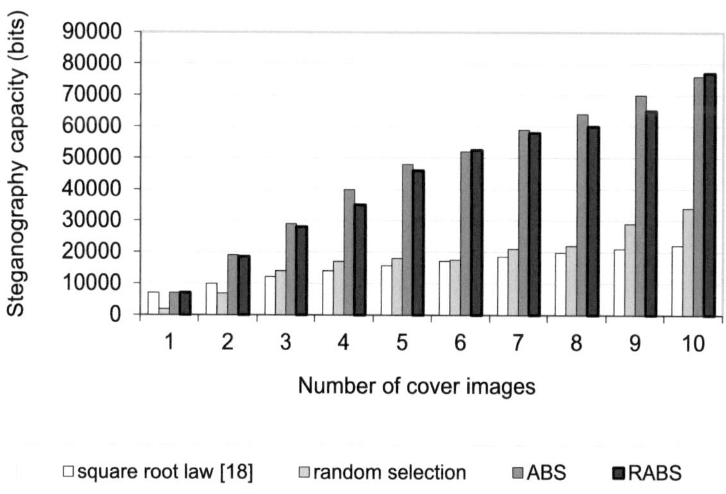

Fig. 3. Relationship between the number of images in cover image sets and total steganography capacity of them when the cover images are selected in random, using ABS, or RABS comparing to square toot law that shows the total steganography capacity in theory.

Figure 3 implies that the square root law of steganographic capacity that is true theoretically, is not always true in practice. We observed that the steganography capacity of a cover image set is approximately a constant, which is multiplied by the number of cover images in the set. In square root law, increasing the number of cover images in a set has a slight influence in total capacity of it. In both ABS and RABS approaches, the total steganography capacity of an image set is approximately the sum of the steganography capacity of all its members.

5. Conclusions

We investigated batch steganography, which is hiding secret data in more than one cover images. This chapter proposes a new adaptive batch steganography approach for hiding a large secret data in multiple cover images by defining and using the steganography capacity of images. Images have various properties due to their different contents. Therefore, for a certain size secret data they could result in stego images with unequal degree of undetectability. In this chapter, we proposed a novel approach to estimate the steganography capacity of images based on signature of clean images, which is achieved by analyzing the similarity between features of cover images. In this regard, an evolutionary fuzzy algorithm is employed to induct fuzzy if-then rules from features of clean images and form the signature of clean images. After discovering the signature of clean images, in the next step, the steganographer can selects the proper cover images from the database. A proper cover image is the one that after embedding, its effective features do not deviate from the signature of clean images. According to the obtained results, our approach reduces the detection rate of steganalyzers compared to the traditional use of steganography methods. The advantage of our proposed approach is that in appearance of new steganalyzer methods, the fuzzy rule base can be upgraded and thus the signature of clean images can become more trustable. By employment of our proposed RABS, one can hide a large secret data securely and quickly in an image set with the least number of images.

6. References

Cachin, C. (1998). An information-theoretic model for steganography, *Proceeding of 2nd Int. Workshop on Information Hiding*, LNCS 1525, pp. 306–318.

Cachin. C. (1998) An information-theoretic model for steganography, *Proceeding of 2nd International Workshop on Information Hiding*, vol. 1525, pp. 306-318.

Cancelli, G.; Doerr, G.; Cox, I. J. & Barni, M. (2008). Detection of ±1 LSB steganography based on the amplitude of histogram local extrema, *Proceeding of International Conference on Image Processing*.

Chandramouli, R. & Memon, N.D. (2003). Steganography Capacity: A Steganalysis Perspective, *Proceeding of SPIE Security and Watermarking of Multimedia Contents*, vol. 5020, pp. 173-177.

Chen, C.; Shi, Y. Q. & Xuan, G. (2006). Statistical Moments Based Universal Steganalysis Using JPEG-2D Array and 2-D Characteristic Function, *Proceeding of International Conference on Image Processing*, pp. 105-108.

Cordon, O.; Gomide, F.; Herrera, F.; Hofmann, F. & Magdalena, L. (2004). Ten years of genetic fuzzy systems current framework and new trends, *Fuzzy Sets and System*, pp. 5–31.

Fridrich, J.; Pevny, T. & Kodovsky, J. (2007). Statistically Undetectable JPEG Steganography: Dead Ends, Challenges, and Opportunities, *Proceeding of ACM Multimedia and Security Workshop*.

Fridrich, J.;Goljan, M. & Soukal, D. (2004). "Perturbed quantization steganography with wet paper codes," Proceeding of ACM, Multimedia Workshop, German.

http://www.cs.washington.edu/research/imagedatabase.
Hu, Y.; Chen, R. & Tzeng, G. (2003). Finding fuzzy classification rules using data mining techniques, *Pattern Recognition Letters*, pp. 509–519.
Ker, A. D. (2006). Batch steganography and pooled steganalysis, *Proceeding of Information Hiding Workshop*, vol. 4437, pp. 265–281.
Ker, A. D. (2007). A Capacity Result for Batch Steganography, *IEEE Signal Processing Let.* vol. 14, no. 8, pp.525-528, 2007
Ker, A. D. (2008). Perturbation Hiding and the Batch Steganography Problem, *Proceeding of 10th Information Hiding Workshop.*
Li, B.;. Shi, Y. Q . & Huang, J. (2008). Steganalysis of YASS, *Proceeding of ACM Multimedia and Security Workshop*, 2008.
Lyu, S. & Farid, H. (2002). Detecting hidden messages using higher-order statistics and support vector machines, *Proceeding of 5th International Workshop on Information Hiding.*
Moulin P. & Mihcak, M. K. (2002). A framework for evaluating the data hiding capacity of image sources, *IEEE Trans. Image Processing*, vol. 11, pp. 1029–1042.
Munuera,C. (2007). Steganography and error-correcting codes, *Signal Processing*, vol. 87, pp. 1528–1533.
Pevný T. & Fridrich, J. (2007). Merging Markov and DCT Features for Multi-Class JPEG Steganalysis, *Proceeding of SPIE, Electronic Imaging, Security, Steganography, and Watermarking of Multimedia Contents.*
Pevny, T. & Fridrich, J. (2008). Novelty Detection in Blind Steganalysis, *Proceeding of ACM Multimedia and Security Workshop*, pp. 167-176.
Pevny, T.; Fridrich, J. & Ker, A.D. (2009). From Blind to Quantities Steganalysis, *Proceeding of SPIE, Electronic Imaging, Security and Forensics of Multimedia Contents*, pp. 0C 1-0C 14.
Sajedi, H. & Jamzad, M. (2008). Adaptive Steganography Method Based on Contourlet Transform, *Proceeding of 9th International Conference on Signal Processing*, pp. 745-748.
Sajedi, H. & Jamzad, M. (2009). Evolutionary Rule Generation for Signature-based Cover Selection Steganography, *Neural Network World*, Special Issue on Intelligent Computing for Multimedia Assurance.
Sajedi, H. & Jamzad, M. (2009). Secure steganography based on embedding capacity, *Journal of Information Security*, Springer, vol. 8, no. 6, pp. 433-445.
Sajedi, H.& Jamzad, M. (2009). ABS: Adaptive batch steganography, *Journal of Optical Engineering*, SPIE Publishing, vol.48, no.8, pp. 087002-1- 087002-10.
Sallee, P. (2003).Model-based steganography, *Proceeding of International Workshop on Digital Watermarking.*
Solanki, K.; Sarkar, A. & Manjunath, B. S. (2007). YASS: yet another steganographic scheme that resists blind steganalysis, *Proceeding of 9th International Workshop on Information Hiding.*
Westfeld, A. (2001). F5-a steganographic algorithm: high capacity despite better steganalysis, *Proceeding of 4th International Workshop on Information Hiding.*

Wu Y. T., & Shih, F. Y. (2006). Genetic Algorithm Based Methodology for Breaking the Steganalytic Systems, *IEEE Transactions on Systems, Man, and Cybernetics-Part B: Cybernetics*, vol. 36, no. 1.

4

Contemporary Approaches to the Histogram Modification Based Data Hiding Techniques

Yildiray Yalman[1], Feyzi Akar[2] and Ismail Erturk[1]
[1]*Turgut Ozal University,*
[2]*Turkish Naval Academy,*
Turkey

1. Introduction

The main objective of this chapter is to present the contemporary approaches to the steganography/data hiding applications, which are based on image histogram modifications. An image histogram is a type of histogram acting as a graphical representation of the tonal distribution in a digital image. The stego images that are produced by using such data hiding techniques are inherently robust against main geometrical attacks such as rotation, scattered tiles and warping, as well as other main attacks. An up-to-date method and its example application to the latest histogram modification based steganography methods and its results are presented in detail and compared to those of the classical ones in the following sections.

Contemporary data hiding applications are usually based on computer software where a vast variety of mathematical algorithms are applied. They have recently made a challenging progress together with the new developments in computer technologies. Quite a lot of data hiding methods and their applications have been proposed since the beginning of 1950s (Cox & Miller, 2002; Ni et al., 2004). However, their initial applications in many areas were unable to ensure a high or required level of information security in time. Thus, both new data hiding techniques and their development have always received ever−increasing interest in parallel to the emerging computer technologies and algorithms (Yalman & Erturk, 2009).

Using data hiding techniques in secret communication purposes has been well proved to be promising. However, a few third parties are usually intended to extract and destroy hidden data (secret bits or stego bits) in cover media in such applications. Most known and easiest of such attacks are lossy compression, LSB changing, cropping, etc. In addition, geometrical attacks have recently appeared to usually change only the pixels' positions of an image, e.g. rotation, scattered tiles and warping. But, these geometrical attacks do not change the image histogram that plots the number of pixels for each tonal value. By looking at the histogram for a specific image, an observer will be able to judge the entire tonal distribution at a glance and he/she can identify unusual situations (comb effect, possibility of hidden data transport etc.) on it. Motivated from these points of view, one of the main objectives of this chapter is to present the contemporary approaches in steganography applications, based on image histogram modifications. The resulting covered/stego images are reasonably robust against main geometrical attacks, which do not change the image histogram, with high quality measurements in terms of human vision system as well as statistically.

Rest of the chapter is organized as follows. Fundamentals of the digital image and image steganography are explained in the following section. Section three details both contemporary approaches to the histogram modification-based data hiding and the HSV method, its implementation, example applications in three well known images together with comparisons to those of the other classical counterparts and its steganalysis. And, final remarks are presented in the last section.

2. The digital image fundamentals and image steganography

2.1 Digital image

A pixel or picture element is the smallest item of information in a digital image (object) that is represented by a series of X rows and Y columns. Pixels are normally arranged in a two-dimensional grid and are often signified using tiny dots, squares, rectangles etc. Each pixel is the smallest sample of an original image (object), where more samples naturally provide more accurate and better demonstrations of the original. The intensity of each pixel is typically variable; for example in color systems, each pixel has classically three or four components, e.g., **RGB** (**R**ed, **G**reen and **B**lue) or **CMYK** (**C**yan, **M**agenta, **Y**ellow and blac**K**) respectively (Sahin et al., 2006; Cetin & Ozcerit, 2009).

Digital images are commonly saved in a grayscale mode in computer systems. The number of bits in order to represent each pixel establishes how many colors or shades of gray are allowed to be displayed. For example, in an 8-bit color mode, the color monitor uses 8 bits for each pixel, allowing displaying 2^8 (256) different colors of gray.

In most cases, many types of differences or deteriorations in numerical values of a digital image cannot be easily perceived by the **H**uman **V**isual **S**ystem (**HVS**) (Fig. 1) which initiates the idea of steganography applications performed through this natural state. In such applications a cover media such as image, video, audio or any other types of multimedia is necessary.

(a) RGB: (197, 100, 45) (b) RGB: (196, 102, 47)

Fig. 1. Magnified original pixel color (a) and stego pixel color deteriorated with hidden data (b).

2.2 Image steganography

Steganography is the art and science of hiding messages or critical information to be relayed. The term steganography is derived from the Greek words steganos (στεγανός) meaning "covered or protected" and graphei (γράφη) meaning "writing". Steganography, therefore, is the all means for covered writing (Fig. 2).

Today, the term steganography states the disguise of secret/critical digital information within computer files. For example, a sender might start with an ordinary−looking digital image file, and then adjust the color of every 10th pixel to correspond to a letter in the alphabet (a change so subtle that anyone, who is not actively or intentionally looking for it, is unlikely to perceive it). It differentiates from the cryptography in that the latter conceals the meaning and content of a secret message, though is unable to conceal the fact that there is a message (Yalman, 2010; Papapanagiotou et al., 2005). Both steganography and cryptography can be combined for optimum and highly reliable communication security (Akar, 2005).

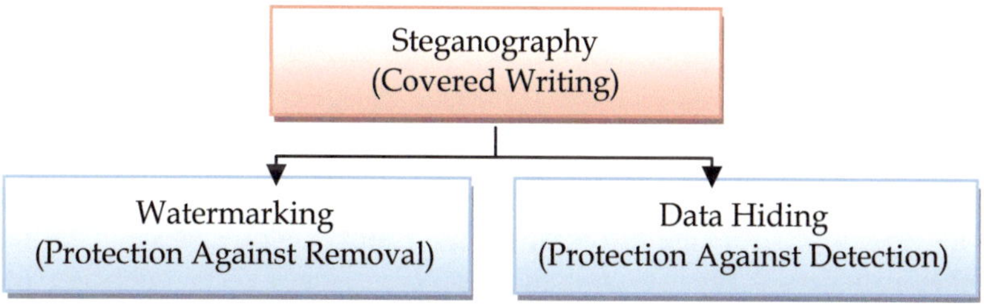

Fig. 2. Directions within steganography methods.

There are a lot of studies about digital image steganography presented in the literature. Almost all of these proposed methods have diverse effects to the image (cover media) due to adding noise or deterioration on it. Although, the HVS is unable to detect these distortions, this situation is totally different, considering the distribution of brightness values on the image histogram. For example, while the HVS cannot sense the differences between images presented in Fig. 3−a and −b (original and stego images) itself, it can easily recognize the difference between their histograms given in Fig. 4−a and −b.

(a) (b)

Fig. 3. Original image (a) and stego image encoded by using LSB−2bits (b).

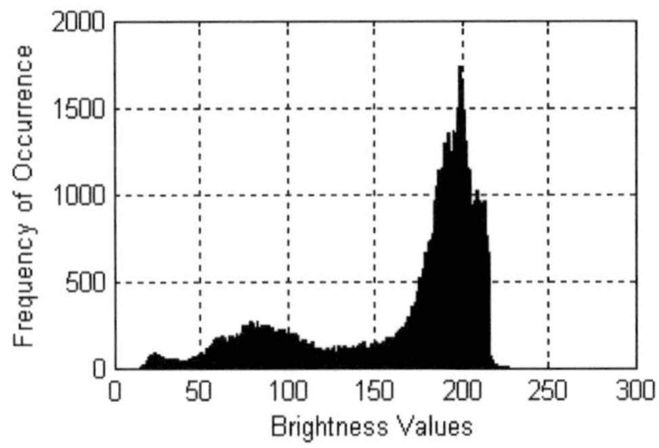

(a)

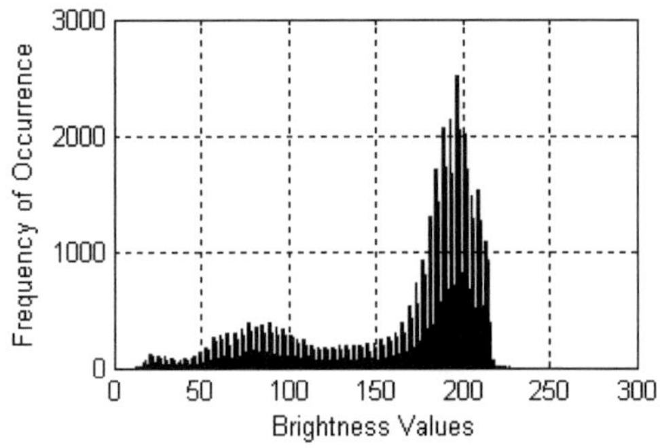

(b)

Fig. 4. Original image (a) and stego image (b) histograms.

This change in the image histograms is called as "comb effect" in literature (Yalman & Erturk, 2009). It basically points out the unbalanced/deteriorated brightness value distribution and may easily lead to the detection of the covered message.

In Fig. 4–a and –b, not only are the image histogram appearances different but also the frequency of occurrence of the brightness values are extremely fluctuated. This natural fact can easily be comprehended by doing a simple check on the stego image histogram without even knowing the original image histogram. As a result one can basically assume that the image had been processed for a reason such as conveying a secret message/information. Regarding all of these important points, histogram–based data hiding applications are highlighted in this chapter because they all aim at producing a stego image histogram without revealing the combing effect.

2.3 Quality measures used in image steganography evaluation

Here **P**eak **S**ignal to **N**oise **R**atio (**PSNR**) and **M**ean **S**quare **E**rror (**MSE**) parameters are considered for statistical analysis of the steganography methods. The MSE should be computed first as given in equation (1) and equation (2) (Sencar et al., 2004) then the PSNR can be derived as in equation (3) (Netravali & Haskell, 1995; Rabbani & Jones, 1991), where "O" and "S" are the original and stego image pixel values (binary) respectively to be compared and the image size is "X × Y". PSNR result of the stego images produced by all of the histogram–based data hiding techniques is guaranteed to be above the other classical techniques' performance in terms of statistical and perceptual invisibility. Note that, equations (1) and (2) are specified for only monochrome images; for color images, the denominator of the equation (3) is multiplied by a factor 3. To compute the PSNR, the block first calculates the mean–squared error using the following equation:

$$MSE = \frac{1}{m \times n} \sum_{i=0}^{m-1} \sum_{j=0}^{n-1} \left\| O(i,j) - S(i,j) \right\|^2 \tag{1}$$

$$MSE = \frac{\sum_{m,n} \left[O(i,j) - S(i,j) \right]^2}{m \times n} \tag{2}$$

$$PSNR = 10\log_{10}\left(\frac{MAX^2}{MSE}\right) \quad (3)$$

Steganography methods and their applications are validated through well–known quality measures. PSNR value is the fundamental metric but it does not match with the HVS exactly. For this reason, different quality measures have been presented and discussed in the literature for the last decade. In addition to PSNR, there are several perceptual measures such as **U**niversal Image **Q**uality **I**ndex (**UQI**) (Wang & Bovik, 2002), **V**isual **I**nformation **F**idelity (**VIF**) (Sheikh & Bovik, 2006) and **M**ean **S**tructural **S**imilarity (**M–SSIM**) (Wang et al., 2004) in order to evaluate and analyze the data hiding methods. The UQI, VIF and the M–SSIM are measured as a quality result (**Q**) that ranges between [–1 and 1], between [0 and 1] and between [0 and 1] respectively, meaning that the best Q value can be 1 for all of them. All of quality measures mentioned above are based upon statistical techniques whose results are compatible with the HVS.

3. Contemporary approaches to the histogram modification–based data hiding

In this section, histogram modification–based data hiding methods presented in the literature are explained. In addition to these, a contemporary method called as HSV, its application and its steganalysis are described in detail.

3.1 Histogram modification–based data hiding

By looking at the histogram of a specific object, an observer would be able to judge the entire tonal distribution of the image at a glance. Histogram modification-based data hiding methods utilize this asset of the digital images to convey any type of secret information.

Ni et al. (2006) initially introduced a histogram based data hiding technique where the crucial information is embedded into the image histogram. Pairs of peak points and zero points are used to achieve low embedding distortion with respect to providing low data hiding capacity. Another histogram modification technique for data hiding has been extensively worked out recently in Fallahpour and Sedaaghi's paper (Fallahpour & Sedaaghi, 2007). It is fundamentally based on block–based. Lee et al. (2006) also proposed a reversible data hiding scheme based on histogram modification of difference images. To increase data hiding ability, Chang et al. (2008) presented an efficient extension of the histogram modification technique by considering the pixel difference instead of simple pixel value and Teng et al. (2010) had some other similar proposals. They also exploited a histogram shifting technique to prevent problems raised about overflow and underflow. Some of these methods are described in the following sub–sections.

3.1.1 Ni et al.'s method

Ni et al. (2006) developed a stimulating algorithm for hiding data in gray level images. The algorithm is based on image histogram modification. If a grayscale image is used as a cover image, firstly, its histogram is generated (Fig. 5 (a)). Moreover, a Peak Point (PP) and a Zero Point (ZP) are determined in the histogram (Fig. 5 (b)). The PP occurs on gray Brightness

Value (BV) 151 and the ZP occurs at 240 as illustrated in Fig. 5 (b). Making the capacity as large as possible is the aim of the discovery of the PP. The number of bits hidden/inserted in the cover image is the same as the number of pixels related to the PP.

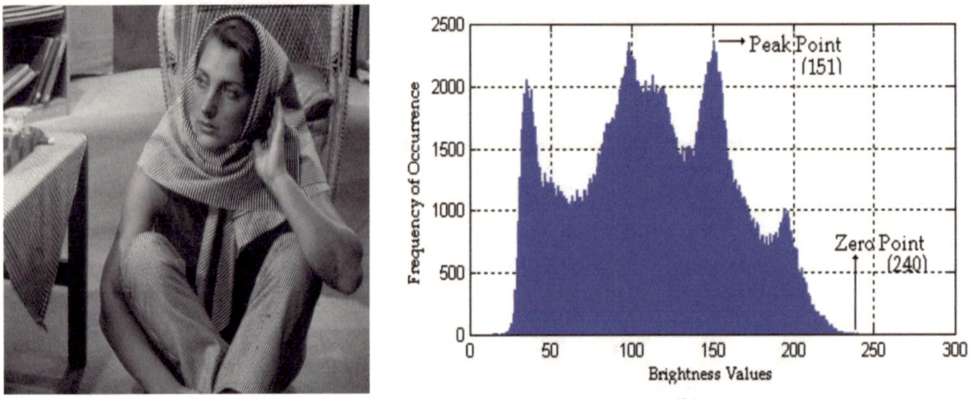

(a) (b)

Fig. 5. The Barbara image (a) and zero point and peak point of its histogram (b).

It is assumed that the PP is less than the ZP. Additionally, the whole cover image is scanned in a specific order (e.g., from top to bottom, right to left). At the first step, the gray BV of the pixels in the range (PP, ZP) is increased by 1. As for the example of the Barbara image, the histogram in the range between 151 (exclusive) and 240 (inclusive) is shifted 1 unit to the right, as demonstrated in Fig. 6.

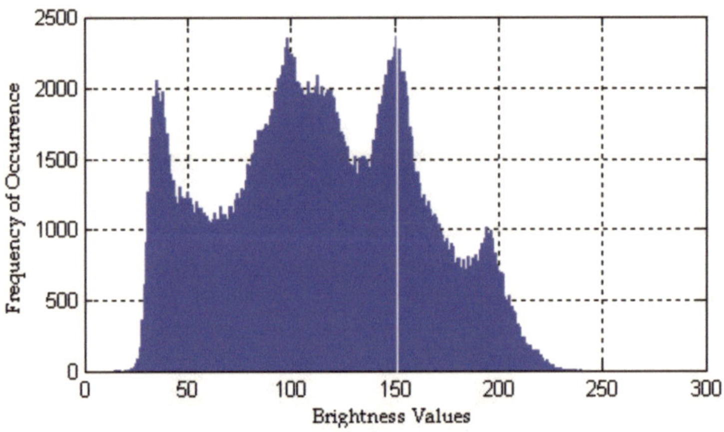

Fig. 6. A crack appears on the original peak BV.

Secondly, the obtained histogram-shifted image is scanned once again in the same order. Once a pixel with gray BV is encountered, the binary sequence of the secret information is explored to be hidden. If the corresponding bit in the sequence is $(1)_2$, the pixel value is increased by 1. Otherwise the pixel brightness value (BV) remains unchanged. As far as the Barbara image in Fig. 5(a) is concerned, it is scanned to seek for the pixels with gray value 151 one at a time. If the corresponding bit in the secret data is binary "1"then the pixel is extended to 152, else it is kept as 151. Finally, the original peak in the histogram is slightly changed as given in Fig. 7.

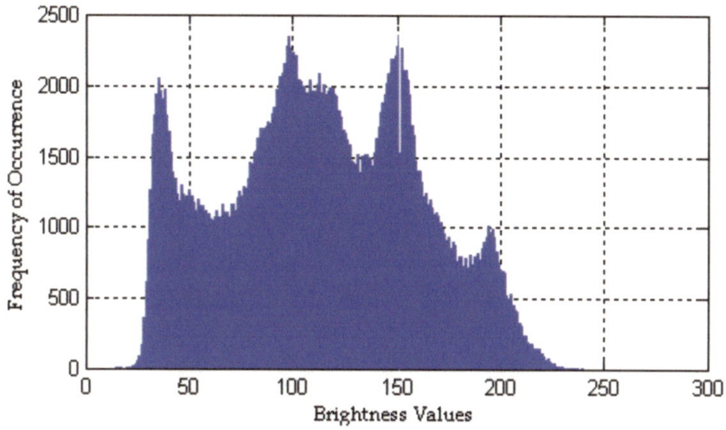

Fig. 7. The histogram after embedding secret data.

When we need to extract the embedded data from the stego-image by using the above algorithm, finding the PP and the ZP are necessary to realize first. Generally, the BVs of PP and ZP are considered as side information and transmitted to the receiver necessarily. In addition, all communication parties are able to modify the BV of the pixel in the specific position, from the upper leftmost pixel to sign PP and ZP in the stego-image.

As a result, the digital images coded by this method cannot be detected by HVS. But steganalysist can still easily notice changes on image histogram because deterioration on its view is marginal as seen in Fig. 7. Above all, Ni et al.'s (2006) method offers very low data embedding capacity making it very unsuitable in current steganography applications.

3.1.2 Teng et al.'s method

Teng et al. (2010) slightly improved Ni et al.'s method detailed above. In accordance with Ni et al.'s method, the data hiding capacity of the cover image directly depends on the frequency of occurrence of the pixels. If it is expected to enhance the data hiding capacity, they offer that they should make more pixels with the BV of the peak. A method to enlarge the number of pixels with the BV of the PP is revealed by taking advantage of the histogram re-quantization.

The histogram quantization is a method in order to reduce the number of bins of the histogram by mapping the pixels into fewer levels. Teng et al. (2010) mapped the pixels in the digital image into 64 levels. Fig. 8 depicts the histogram of the Barbara image with 64 levels based on histogram re-quantization.

Comparing Fig. 8 to Fig. 5 (b), the frequency of occurrence of pixels in peak increases more than 2 times. The hidden data is to be concealed in these pixels. The encoding steps of the Teng et al.'s (2010) data embedding algorithm are given as follows:

1. Assume that D is the difference between two nearest signified gray levels as the total number of bins and generate the histogram of the cover image in 256/D levels.
2. Find the peak bin [PP, PP+D) and the zero bin [ZP, ZP+D) in the histogram.
3. If PP<ZP then a pixel with gray BV in the range of [PP+D, ZP) is increased by D. Afterwards, the cover image is scanned in the given order and the pixels with gray BV in the range [PP, PP+D) are increased by D if its corresponding bit in the secret data is binary "1". If PP>ZP, then a pixel with gray BV in the range of [ZP+D, PP) is decreased by D. Afterwards, the cover image is scanned in the given order and the pixels with gray BV in the range (PP−D, PP] are reduced by D if its corresponding bit in the data is binary "1".
4. Get the stego−image and relay it to the receiver.

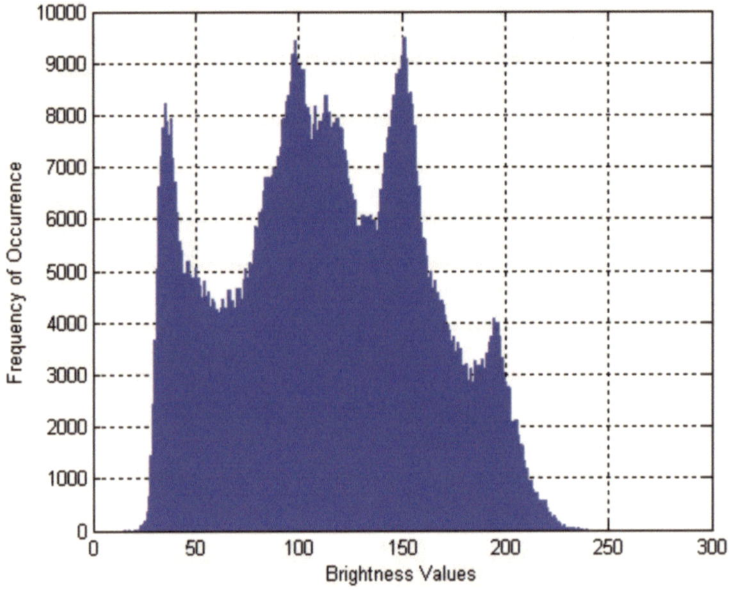

Fig. 8. The histogram of the Barbara image with 64 levels.

According to the Teng et al.'s (2010) method, the value of 4 or 8 is recommended for D because the image quantized into 64 or 32 levels is generally lossless for HVS.

Data extracting part of algorithm are given as follows:

1. The stego−image is scanned in the same given order.
2. The pixel with gray BV [PP, PP+D) indicates the corresponding data bit is 0.
3. If PP<ZP, then a pixel with gray BV [PP+D, PP+2D) indicates the corresponding data bit is 1.
   If PP>ZP, then a pixel with gray BV [PP−D, PP) indicates the corresponding data bit is 1.
4. Get the hidden embedded data.

This method offers more capacity than Ni et al.'s method but it still offers small capacity and unacceptably low PSNR values according to the other histogram based data hiding approaches.

3.1.3 Krishna et al.'s method

Krishna et al.'s (2010) introduced another histogram based data hiding algorithm too. However it is a reversible data hiding technique based on histogram modification using pairs of PP and ZPs has the process of adding '1', if peak BV of pixel has been encountered. Otherwise, '0' is added, i.e. if zero is detected. From this they can estimate the number of pixels in the image with peak BVs. However, for an unusual image with equal histogram, with this technique minimum points can be embedded. Also the peak and minimum points should be requirement of the receiver for full recovering.

As an alternative to using pixel BV, the differences between neighbor pixels are considered; they get the differences have almost a zero−mean and a Laplacian−like distribution. Although this leads to a partial improvement in data embedding ability, still the PP pairs are tallied to the receiver. To demonstrate the method, consider an 8−bit grayscale cover image with a pixel BV, x_i denoting the grayscale BV of ith pixel (between 0 and 255). The image is scanned in inverse s−order and the differences between neighbor pixels are calculated. By determining the PP from the pixel differences, another scan is realized on whole image in inverse s-order as previously.

If the difference is higher than the peak BV, the secret data bit cannot be embedded so x_i is shifted by 1 unit. However, for the pixel difference is less than the peak BV, a secret data bit is embedded. At the receiver side, the whole image is scanned in the given same order and the secret data bit is extracted from the stego image. Here Krishna et al.'s (2010) suggests using only one PP for data hiding. For large data embedding capacities above process is reiterated and the PPs to be noted for every hiding pass. In order to correspond the multiple PPs, a binary tree structure is designed as presented in Fig. 9.

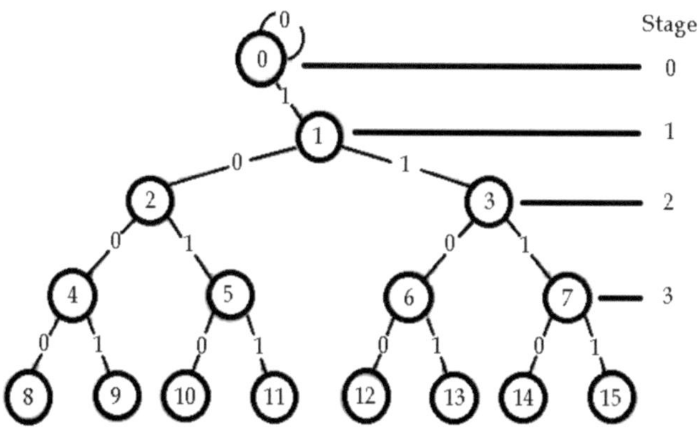

Fig. 9. The binary tree structure.

PPs are assumed to be 2^S for embedding secret data, where S is a stage of binary tree. Here each node is a PP. If the pixel difference is less than the peak BV, secret data bit can be embedded. If '0' bit to be added, the left sub-node is visited otherwise the right sub-node is visited. Employing this method the payloads are increased; tree stages are also increased in turn image distortion is increased too. All recipients need to share with sender its tree stage S, because this tree establishes multiple PPs. If the difference is higher than the peak BV secret data bit cannot be embedded so x_i is shifted by 1 unit. However, for pixel difference less than the peak BV, a secret data bit is embedded. At the receiver side, the whole image is scanned in the same order and the secret data bit is extracted from the stego image (Krishna et al.'s, 2010).

Pixels are modified in the above process, which might lead to overflow or underflow. Krishna et al. (2010) suggest narrowing the histogram from both sides to avoid overflow and underflow. So the method shifts both sides by 2^S units meaning that the histogram is narrowed in the range 2^S, $255-2^S$. The histogram shifting information is recorded as overhead book maintaining information that has to be hidden into the cover image itself with payload.

Data embedding and extracting algorithms of the Krishna et al.'s method are as follows:

a. **Embedding process:**

An N−pixel 8−bit grayscale image with pixel value x_i (between 0 and 255) is considered for embedding process (Krishna et al.'s, 2010).

1. Find the stage S of the binary tree. S determines the data embedding capacity.
2. Histogram is shifted from both sides narrowing in the range 2^S, $255-2^S$, still maintaining the shifting information in the payload.
3. Scan the entire image in an inverse s−order and find differences between neighbor pixel BVs.
4. Again scan the entire image in inverse s−order. Determine if x_i should be shifted by 2^S.
5. If the difference is less than 2^S, embed a secret data bit with x_i.

b. **Extraction process:**

At receiver side hidden data is extracted from the stego image and the original image is recovered with the help of S stage of a binary tree (Krishna et al.'s, 2010).

1. Scan the stego image in inverse s−order.
2. Calculate the differences to extract the embedded secret data bits.
3. Recover original cover image by shifting in the reverse order as done during the data embedding process.
4. Repeat step 2 until the embedded secret data is fully extracted.
5. Extract the overhead information from the extracted secret data.

3.2 A contemporary histogram modification−based data hiding method: HSV

The HSV method differs from the existing histogram−based data hiding methods regarding the following two important aspects. First of all, stego images and their histograms cannot be detected by the HVS. Secondly, data hiding capacity is comparatively higher than the other methods. Its algorithm can be easily applied because it is too simple. Following sub−sections detail the method.

3.2.1 HSV method

This part is mainly based on Yalman & Erturk's method (Yalman & Erturk, 2009) that is shortly called in (Yalman, 2010) as **HSV (H**istogram based **S**teganography on **V**ideo**)**. In this scheme, the HSV approach mainly utilizes the LSB secret data embedding technique and histogram processing.

The HSV and its algorithm principally modify a cover image's histogram for data hiding where neither the resulting new stego image nor its histogram is noticeably different from the original. Therefore, they are both perceived exactly same as the original ones by the HVS (Human Visual System). The HSV method considers the **F**requency of **O**ccurrence (**FO**) of the pixel **B**rightness **V**alues (**BVs**) of the cover image, and then the data hiding process is realized based upon it. First of all, the cover image histogram is produced where the lowest and the highest BVs are determined and named as the Lowest **B**rightness **V**alue (**LBV**) and the **U**pper **B**rightness **V**alue (**UBV**), respectively. These two margins are used to indicate where the process of data hiding could be accomplished (Fig. 10). The idea of the HSV and its implementation processes are explained with an example as follows;

Let's assume the first three stego bits of the secret data are $(010)_2$ and the cover image's histogram produced is given as in the Fig. 10 where the FOs of the LBV (i.e., 22), 23 and 24 BVs are "6", "18" and "31" (Table 1).

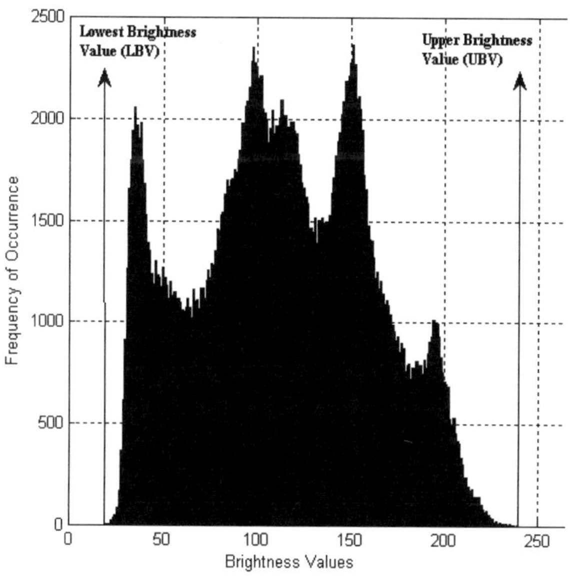

Fig. 10. Determining the LBV and UBV of an image histogram.

Brightness Values (BVs)	22	23	24
Frequency of Occurrence (FOs) of the BVs	6	18	31

Table 1. The first three BVs and their FOs.

At the first step, the algorithm takes that the first stego bit is "0" and the FO of the LBV is 6. Then it computes the Mod2 of this FO as "0" (6 Mod2 = 0). After that, whether the stego bit and the Mod2 process result are equal is checked. If so, as in this example (i.e., 0 = 0), the BV remains as it is (i.e., 22) meaning that it contains now the stego bit "0".

It then proceeds with the following second stego bit "1" and the FO (i.e., 18) of the next BV (i.e., 23) as the second step. Similar to the previous step, the algorithm computes the Mod2 of this FO as "0" (18 Mod2 = 0). After that, whether the stego bit and the Mod2 process result are equal is checked. Since they are not equal (i.e., $1 \neq 0$), now one pixel of the image, whose BV is 23, is changed to the next following BV (i.e., 24). Thus, the resulting FOs of the BV(23) and BV(24) are changed to "17" and "32" respectively, which means that the new FO of the BV(23) contains now the second stego bit "1" (Table 2).

These two processes are applied for the following stego bits and the FOs of the BVs repeatedly until all of the stego bits are embedded in or the UBV is reached indicating the full image data hiding capacity is already utilized.

Brightness Values (BVs)	22	23	24
Frequency of Occurrence (FOs) of the BVs	6	17	32

Table 2. The first three BVs and their FOs after completing $(010)_2$ hiding processes.

The HSV fundamentally differs from the well-known LSB data hiding method, where the least significant bits of the digitalized values of the pixels are modified, in that the frequency of occurrence of the cover image brightness values are modified to embed secret data in. It intrinsically overcomes the salt & pepper effect (Ni et al., 2008) as the boundaries of the resulting brightness values of the stego image are always between "0" and "255". In addition, considering its usage in 24-bit RGB color images (i.e., producing three different histograms for the R, G and B channels of each pixel) separately, a much higher data hiding capacity is well achievable. Another outstanding aspect of the HSV is about dynamically increasing the data embedding capacity (if required), well trading off the PSNR results insignificantly. This is easily achievable dividing the cover image into multiple parts and then applying the method to each part concurrently (Yalman & Erturk, 2009).

Obtaining the stego bits from the stego image using the HSV is much easier than the above secret data embedding process. Initially the stego image histogram is obtained for the secret data extraction process and the LBV & UBV of the histogram are determined. After that the Mod2 process is realized starting from the FO of LBV (i.e., "6" in the example), which is repeated until the UBV is reached in the histogram (Yalman & Erturk, 2009). Considering the data hiding example, following processes explain revealing the stego bits (i.e., "$(010)_2$") extracted from the stego image histogram values (Table II). Thus the stego bits are calculated as follows;

$$\left.\begin{array}{c} 6 \text{ Mod2} = 0 \\ 17 \text{ Mod2} = 1 \\ 32 \text{ Mod2} = 0 \end{array}\right\} \longrightarrow (010)_2$$

3.2.2 Example HSV applications and comparative analysis of the results

Experimental visual results of the HSV approach on the well-known images Lena, Baboon and Peppers are displayed in Fig. 11 (Yalman & Erturk, 2009). The visual differences between the original cover images (i.e., Fig. 11-a, -b and -c) and the corresponding stego images with random hidden data (i.e., Fig. 11–d, –e and –f) can be hardly detected by the human eyes (i.e., the HVS). This is the most important of any steganography application, well achieved by using the HSV.

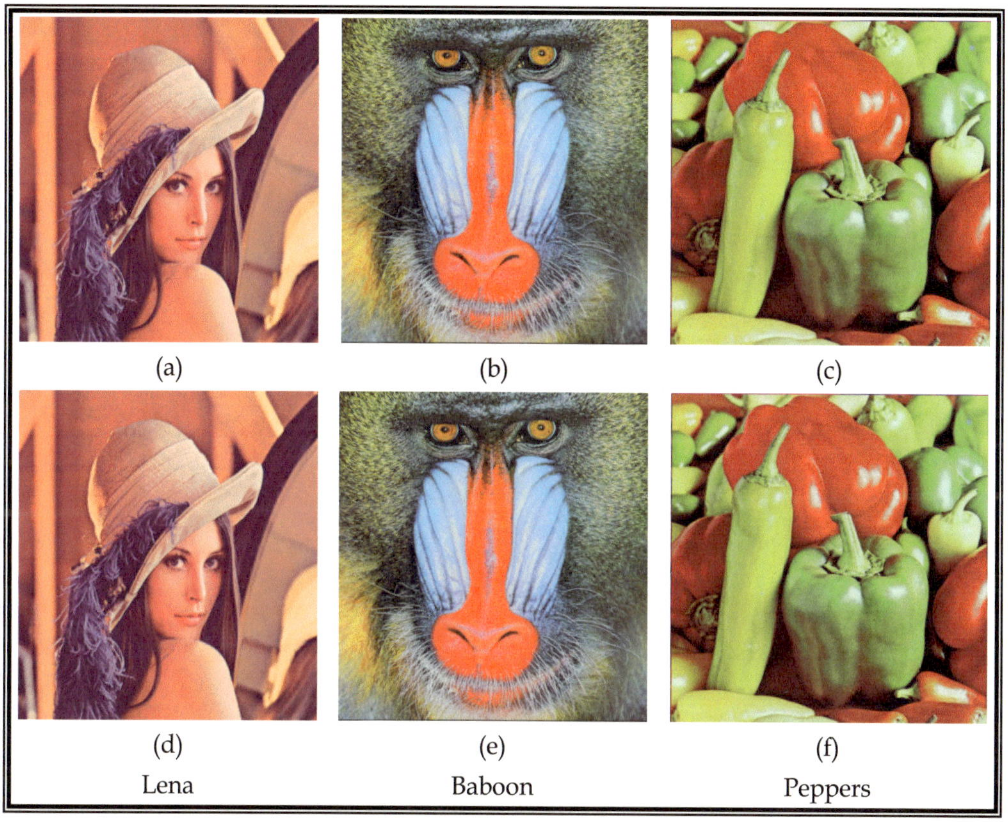

Fig. 11. Original cover images (a–b–c) and the HSV stego images (d–e–f).

The differences among the original, HSV stego and a classical stego images can be realized by the HVS when images are enlarged/magnified highly (Fig. 12). In Fig. 12–c the picture contains more hidden data but this result is not enough due to the fact that the distortion on Lena image is noticeable and this is unacceptable for the users.

Fig. 13 shows the most crucial and valuable aspect of the HSV, in which the Lena is utilized as the cover image as an example. Fig. 13–a, –b and –c are the original cover image R, G and B histograms respectively. Fig 13–d, –e and –f are the stego image R, G and B histograms obtained from the resulting stego image applying the HSV while Fig. 13–g, –h and -i belong to the stego image R, G and B histograms obtained from the resulting stego image applying another traditional method (Yalman & Erturk, 2009). It is clearly understood that there is almost no change on the R, G and B histograms as a result of utilizing the HSV with respect to their original histograms. Moreover, the HVS cannot sense the changes resulted from the data hiding process. On the other hand, many of the classical data hiding algorithms result in highly fluctuating and combing changes in the stego histograms, for instance in the RWB technique (e.g., Fig. 13–g, –h and –i) (Akar & Varol, 2004).

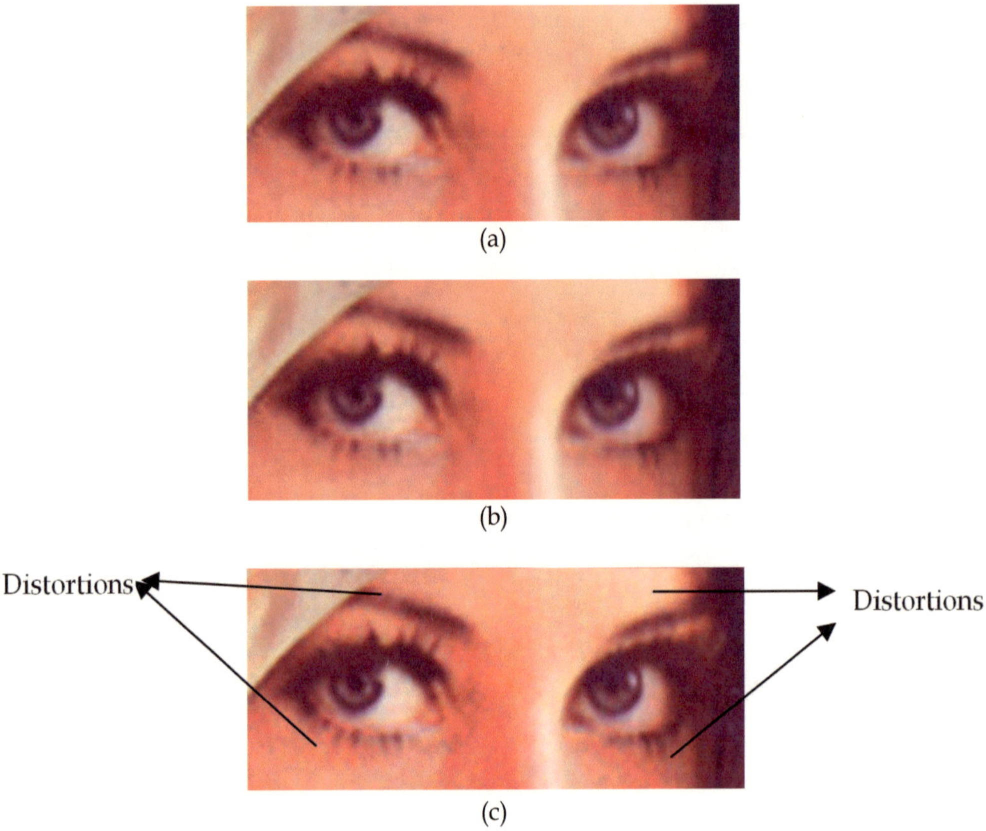

Fig. 12. Original and marked "Lena" images; original (a), coded by HSV (b), coded by classical RGB weight based (RWB) encoding technique (c).

Another important issue in comparing the HSV data hiding approach with its counterparts (e.g., presented in Chrysochos et al.'s (2007) paper that is also based on histogram modifications) that produce almost all the same stego image histograms as HSV does is the PSNR performance with respect to the maximum secret data embedding capacity.

The HSV always results in better PSNR values as well as doubles the data embedding capacity compared to those of Chrysochos' algorithm (Table 3, Table 4). It should be noted

	Chrysochos et al.'s (2007)		**HSV**	
	PSNR (dB)	*Embedded Data (Bits)*	*PSNR (dB)*	*Embedded Data (Bits)*
Lena	54.12	360	62.75	665
Baboon	53.10	300	59.25	747
Peppers	55.18	300	56.01	700

Table 3. Experimental results for different images and embedded bits (Yalman & Erturk, 2009).

that the maximum secret data embedding capacity of the HSV is directly related to the difference between the UBV and the LBV. Therefore, it is a very clear fact that HSV is mostly suited to the cover images with brightness value histograms uniformly distributed from "0" to "255" with respect to data embedding capacity.

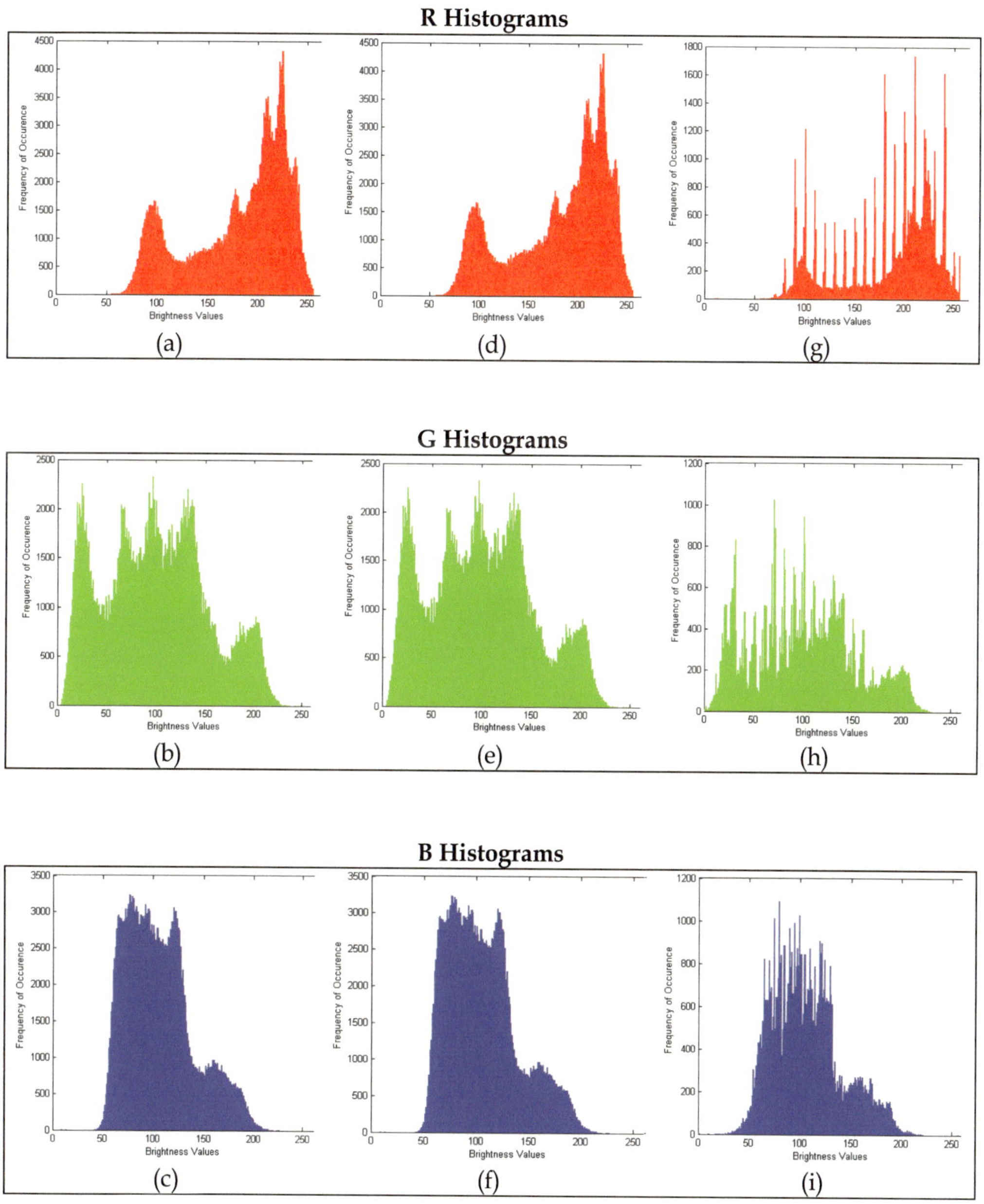

Fig. 13. The original Lena R–G–B histograms (a–b–c) and their stego image counterparts applying both HSV (d–e–f) and the RWB (g–h–i).

	Embedded Data (bits)	**Chrysochos et al.'s (2007)**	**HSV**
		PSNR (dB)	*PSNR (dB)*
Lena	360	54.12	72.59
Baboon	300	53.10	84.81
Peppers	300	55.18	80.84

Table 4. Comparisons of PSNR results for the same data embedding capacity (Yalman, 2010).

As mentioned above, only a PSNR analysis is not adequate for a complete quality assessment of any steganography method. In addition to PSNR; VIF, UQI and M-SSIM visual quality measures are also used for the performance comparisons in this chapter (Table 5). Considering these parameters, the HSV method gives results that are closer the finest quality (about 1).

	RWB	**LSB (2bits)**	**LSB**	**HSV**	**RWB**	**LSB (2bits)**	**LSB**	**HSV**
	Lena				**Baboon**			
VIF	0.9798	0.9802	0.9981	**0.9993**	0.9823	0.9888	0.9930	**0.9997**
UQI	0.9237	0.9440	0.9988	**0.9995**	0.9724	0.9814	0.9945	**0.9998**
M-SSIM	0.9531	0.9654	0.9991	**0.9997**	0.9801	0.9890	0.9980	**0.9999**
	Peppers				**Airplane**			
VIF	0.9573	0.9786	0.9980	**0.9998**	0.9571	0.9325	0.9976	**0.9997**
UQI	0.9012	0.9435	0.9976	**0.9999**	0.8375	0.9390	0.9950	**0.9997**
M-SSIM	0.9366	0.9703	0.9986	**0.9999**	0.9422	0.9612	0.9980	**0.9998**

Table 5. Experimental results for different statistical metrics for different 512×512 gray images coded by using four steganography methods.

The data hiding capacity of the HSV can be improved by applying a histogram stretching technique (or histogram equalization) that consequently increases the difference between the LBV and the UBV of an image histogram or HSV can be applied in small pieces of image to increase the capacity (Fig. 14). If the method is applied onto the well decided pieces of the cover image, it will increase the payload size exponentially as the results in Fig. 15 show it clearly.

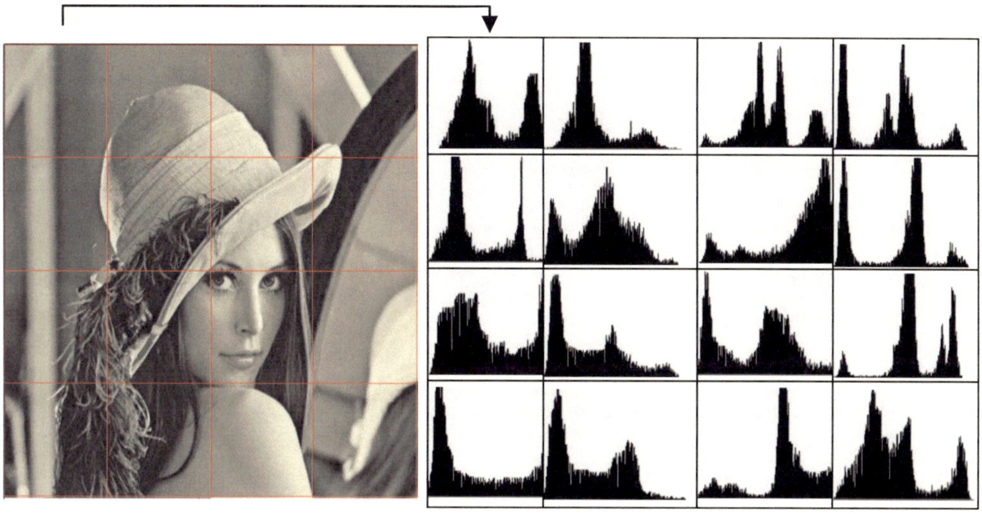

(a) (b)

Fig. 14. Implementation of the HSV to small parts (b) of the image (a).

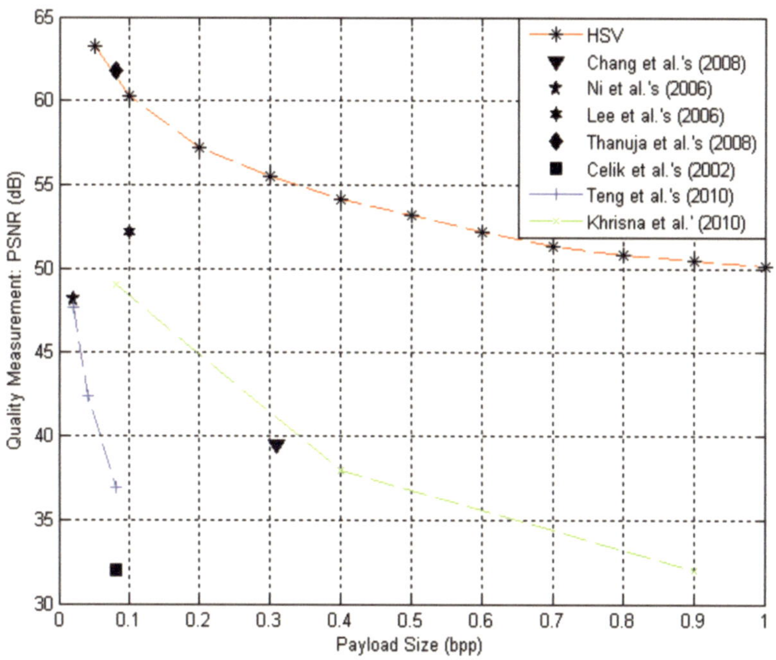

Fig. 15. PSNR versus payload size for test image Lena (512×512).

In addition to the above distinguishing results, the HSV is also uniquely strong against geometric attacks like the other classical histogram based steganography methods. The geometric attacks usually change the pixel positions of a digital image, but unable to effect the image histogram. Based on this fact, the HSV is clearly defiant to such attacks as rotation, scattering tiles, warping etc. (Fig. 16).

(a) Scattered Tiles (b) Rotation (45°) (c) Warping

Fig. 16. Main geometrical attacks against a stego image (Peppers).

3.2.3 Steganalysis of the HSV

In this sub-section, the HSV method is studied using three well-known steganalysis methods that are namely the Raw-Quick-Pairs (RQP), Stegdetect Tool and Visual Steganalysis. The primary objective of any steganographic method is to cover and transmit secret information within a cover image (Lin et al., 2008). If this fact is probable for an attacker to find out or to realize that a cover image has hidden information then thisobjective of the data hiding method is failed. Such type of attacks is called as detection attacks (Fridrich et al., 2000).

The RQP steganalysis method is fundamentally based on statistics of the numbers of unique colors and close-color couples in a 24-bit RGB image (Fridrich et al., 2000). A couple of colors are defined as close if

$$|R_1 - R_2| \leq 1,\ |G_1 - G_2| \leq 1 \text{ and } |B_1 - B_2| \leq 1. \tag{4}$$

When data are embedded into a digital cover image using the LSB-based data hiding technique, the number of unique colors U generally increases so that the following measure will increase (Fridrich et al., 2000):

$$Q = \frac{P}{\binom{U}{2}} \tag{5}$$

where P is the number of close-color pairs and the number of all possible color pairs/couples in the color palette. If the cover image already contains a hidden message and after embedding a known new data on top of it, the difference between the Q_1 and the Q_2 values is marginally small (e.g., less than 0.009). Otherwise, a high variation between the Q_1 and the Q_2 values above 0.01 means that the steganography method producing the stego image is confirmed (Sahin et al., 2007). Thus, it is easily possible to sense the occurrence of a secret data by adding a test data into a stego image and observing the amount of variation in Q .

Three different stego images (Fig. 11−d, −e, −f) that are produced by using the HSV are evaluated using the RQP method and the results are presented in Table 6. Easily understood from all of the examples, the variation in Q values of the stego images and the stego images with test data ($|Q_1 - Q_2|$) are such high that one could not realize the existence of the hidden data in the cover images, justifying and validating the HSV method.

Stego image	Q_1 (for the stego image)	Q_2 (for the stego image with test data)	$\|Q_1 - Q_2\|$
Lena	0.24621	0.22568	0.02053
Baboon	0.40172	0.38625	0.01547
Peppers	0.31940	0.30851	0.01089

Table 6. RQP steganalysis of the HSV.

Robustness of the HSV is also checked using a software tool called as Stegdetect (OutGuess Steganography Detection Tool). The output from the Stegdetect lists either a steganographic application found in the cover image or "negative" if no steganographic substance could be detected. The results for the three stego images given in Fig. 11−d, −e, −f) are all obtained as negative as given in Table 7. Therefore this second method also well confirms the use of HSV and its consistency.

Stego image	Stegdetect Result
Lena	Negative
Baboon	Negative
Peppers	Negative

Table 7. Stegdetect steganalysis of the HSV.

Since human beings have really sophisticated pattern recognition capabilities that are mainly optimized for images, one possibility is that they will be superior to the other classical techniques (e.g., RQP and Stegdetect), and human visual observation may succeed where steganalysis methods based on statistical analysis are not successful (Watters et al., 2005). In order to justify the superiority of the HSV, an output stego image and the original cover image are depicted in Fig. 17 for visual observation. Having done many ordinary user visual tests, none has come up with the conclusion that the figures are different in anyhow.

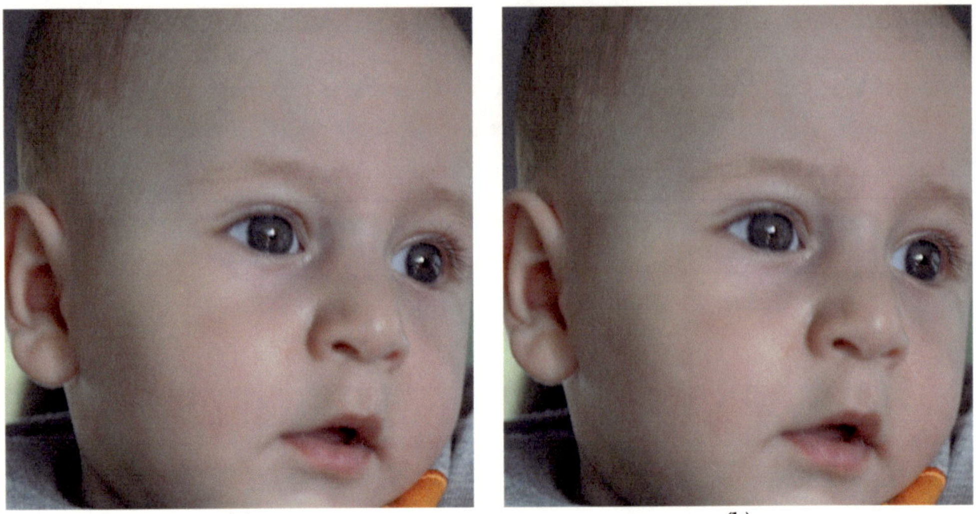

(a) (b)

Fig. 17. An example of HSV output stego image (b) and original cover image (a) for human visual observation test.

4. Conclusions

In this chapter, the histogram-based steganography, classical and contemporary approaches and their advantages are presented. These advantages can be summarized as follows; relatively high data hiding capacity, imperceptibility on stego image and its histogram, high statistical quality for stego images not only in terms of PSNR but also VIF, UQI and M-SSIM, applicable to very small digital images and robust against geometrical attacks.

A contemporary histogram-based data hiding approach (HSV), its applications and evaluations are also given in detail. Application and experimental results of the HSV for well-known test images Lena, Baboon and Peppers clearly show that the visual differences between the original and the corresponding stego images with random hidden data cannot be detected by the human visual system. As a concluding final remark, the original image histogram is almost same as the resulting stego image histogram produced by using the HSV; thus, neither visual nor statistical comparison of them (assuming that the attacker has the original image and its histogram although this is an extremely difficult case) enables perception of any data hiding application being realized. All of these results confirm the success of histogram-based approaches to data hiding over classical methods.

5. References

Akar, F. & Varol, H.S. (2004). A New RGB Weighted Encoding Technique for Efficient Information Hiding in Images. *Journal of Naval Science and Engineering*, vol. 2, July 2004, pp. 21–36.

Akar, F. (2005). Implementation of Information Security Based on Steganography and Cryptology. *Marmara University, PhD. Thesis*, 2005.

Celik, M. U.; Sharma, G.; Tekalp, A. M. & Saber, E. (2002). Reversible Data Hiding, *IEEE International Conference of Image Processing*, vol. 2, pp. 157–160, 2002.

Cetin, O. & Ozcerit, A. T. (2009). A New Steganography Algorithm Based on Color Histograms for Data Embedding into Raw Video Streams. *Computers & Security*, 2009, pp. 670-682.

Chang, C. C.; Tai, W. L. & Chen, K. N. (2008). Lossless Data Hiding Based on Histogram Modification for Image Authentication, *IEEE/IFIP International Conference on Embedded and Ubiquitous Computing*, pp. 506–511, 2008.

Chrysochos, E.; Fotopoulos, V.; Skodras, A. & Xenos, M. (2007). Reversible Image Watermarking Based on Histogram Modification, *11th Conference on Informatics with International Participation*, vol. B, pp. 93-104, Greece, 2007.

Cox, I. J. & Miller, M. L. (2002). The First 50 Years of Electronic Watermarking. *Journal of Applied Signal Processing*, vol. 16, no. 4, 2002, pp. 126-132.

Fallahpour, M. & Sedaaghi, M. H. (2007). High Capacity Lossless Data Hiding Based on Histogram Modification. *IEICE Electronics Express*, vol. 4, no. 7, 2007, pp. 205–210.

Fridrich, J.; Du, R. & Long, M. (2000). Steganalysis of LSB Encoding in Color Images, *IEEE Int. Conf. on Multimedia and Expo (ICME)*, vol. 3, pp. 1279–1282, 2000.

Krishna, S. L. V.; Rahim, B. A.; Shaik, F. & Rajan, K. S. (2010). Lossless Embedding Using Pixel Differences and Histogram Shifting Technique, *IEEE Recent Advances in Space Technology Services and Climate Change (RSTSCC)*, pp. 213–216, 2010.

Lee, S. K.; Suh, Y. H. & Ho, Y. S. (2006). Reversible Image Authentication Based on Watermarking, *IEEE International Conference on Multimedia and Expo*, Canada, pp. 1321–1324, 2006.

Lin, C. Y.; Chang, C. C. & Wang, Y. Z. (2008). Reversible Steganographic Method with High Payload for JPEG Images, *IEICE Transactions on Information and Systems*, vol. E91.D, no. 3, 2008, pp. 836–845.

Netravali A. N. & Haskell, B. G. (1995). *Digital Pictures: Representation, Compression and Standards*, Plenum Press, New York, 1995.

Ni, Z.; Shi, Y. Q.; Ansari, N.; Su, W.; Sun, Q. & Lin, X. (2004). Robust Lossless Image Data Hiding, *IEEE Int. Conference on Multimedia and Expo (ICME)*, pp. 2199-2202, 2004.

Ni, Z.; Shi, Y. Q.; Ansari, N. & Su, W. (2006). Reversible Data Hiding. *IEEE Transactions on Circuits and Systems for Video Technology*, vol. 16, no. 3, Mar. 2006, pp. 354–362.

Ni, Z.; Shi, Y. Q.; Ansari, N.; Su, W., Sun, Q. & Lin, X. (2008). Robust Lossless Image Data Hiding Designed for Semi–Fragile Image Authentication. *IEEE Transactions on Circuits and Systems for Video Technology*, vol. 18, no. 4, 2008, pp. 497-509.

OutGuess Steganography Detection Tool: (http://www.outguess.org/detection.php, accessed August 9, 2011.

Papapanagiotou, K.; Kelliniz, E.; Marias, G. F. & Georgiadis, P. (2005). Alternatives for Multimedia Messaging System Steganography, *Lecture Notes in Computer Science, Computational Intelligence and Security*, vol. 3802, pp. 589-596, 2005.

Rabbani, M. & Jones, P. W. (1991). *Digital Image Compression Techniques*, SPIE Optical Engineering Press, Washington, 1991.

Sahin, A.; Bulus, E. & Sakalli, M. T. (2006). LSB Data Hiding on 24 Bits RGB Images. *Trakya University Journal of Science*, 2006, pp. 17-22.

Sahin, A.; Bulus, E.; Sakalli, M. T. & Bulus, H. N. (2007). The Grasp of the Hidden Information on Images With the RQP Steganalysis Method", *IXth Akademik Bilisim Conferences*, pp. 83–87, 2007.

Sencar, H. T.; Ramkumar, M. & Akansu, A. N. (2004). *Data Hiding Fundamentals and Applications*, Elsevier Academic Press, New York, 2004.

Sheikh, H. D. & Bovik, A. C. (2006). Image Information and Visual Quality. *IEEE Transactions on Image Processing*, vol. 15, 2006, pp. 430–444.

Teng, C. Y.; Shiau, Y. H. & Chen, C. C. (2010). A Data Hiding Algorithm Based on Histogram Re–quantization, *IEEE 5th International Conference on Computer Sciences and Convergence Information Technology (ICCIT)*, pp. 1088–1091, 2010.

Thanuja, T. C.; Nagaraj, R. & Kumari, M. U. (2008). Reversible Data Hiding Using Increased Peak Histogram, *IEEE Proceedings of International Workshop on Data Mining and Artificial Intelligence (DMAI' 08)*, pp.44–47, 2008.

Wang, Z. & Bovik, A.C. (2002). A Universal Image Quality Index. *IEEE Signal Processing Letters*, vol. 9, 2002, pp. 81–84.

Wang, Z.; Bovik, A. C.; Sheikh, H.D. & Simoncelli, E.P. (2004). Image Quality Assessment: From Error Visibility To Structural Similarity. *IEEE Transactions on Image Processing*, vol. 13, 2004, pp. 600–612.

Watters, P. A.; Martin, F. & Stripf, H. S. (2005). Visual Steganalysis of LSB–Encoded Natural Images, *Proc. of the IEEE 3rd International Conference on Information Technology and Applications (ICITA'05)*, vol. 1, pp. 746–751, 2005.

Yalman, Y. & Erturk, I. (2009). A New Histogram Modification Based Robust Image Data Hiding Technique, *IEEE 24th Int. Symposium on Computer and Information Sciences (ISCIS'09)*, pp.39–43, 2009.

Yalman, Y. (2010). Design and Implementation of A Steganography Method Based on Histogram Modification for Digital Images. *PhD. Thesis*, Kocaeli University, 2010.

5

Lossless Steganography for Speech Communications

Naofumi Aoki
Graduate School of Information Science and Technology, Hokkaido University
Japan

1. Introduction

Transmitting supplementary data by steganography, new functions can be added to communications systems without changing conventional data format. Based on this concept, several applications have been proposed for enhancing the speech quality of telephony communications. These applications secretly transmit side information along with speech data itself for enhancing the performance of signal processing such as packet loss concealment and band extension (Aoki, 2003; Aoki, 2006; Aoki, 2007a; Aoki, 2012).

The simplest steganography technique employed in such applications is the LSB (Least Significant Bit) replacement technique (Cox, 2008). It just replaces the LSB of speech data with secret message. Since the LSB of speech data is not very important in perception, the LSB replacement technique is sufficient enough in many practical cases.

However, there is no way to avoid inevitable degradation of speech data by embedding secret message with the LSB replacement technique. In order to mitigate this problem, this article describes an idea of the lossless steganography technique for telephony communications (Aoki, 2007b; Aoki, 2008; Aoki, 2009a; Aoki, 2009b; Aoki, 2010a). The proposed technique exploits the characteristic of the folded binary code employed in several speech codecs, such as G.711 and DVI-ADPCM.

2. LSB replacement technique

The LSB replacement technique is known as one of the simplest steganography technique (Cox, 2008). It just embeds secret message into the LSB of cover data. The embedding procedure of the LSB replacement technique is programmed in C language as shown in Fig. 1. In this procedure, b represents a 1 bit secret message and c represents an 8bit cover data. The LSB replacement technique is categorized as a lossy steganography technique, since it may degrade cover data by embedding secret message.

```
if (b == 0) c &= 0xFE;
if (b == 1) c |= 0x01;
```

Fig. 1. Embedding procedure of the LSB replacement technique programmed in C language.

3. Lossless steganography technique based on the folded binary code

For representing signed integers as binary data, many speech codecs employ the folded binary code instead of the 2's complement, the most common format of binary data. Table 1 shows how an 8 bit speech data is represented by the folded binary code as well as the 2's complement.

decimal number	2's complement	folded binary code
+127	0 1 1 1 1 1 1 1	0 1 1 1 1 1 1 1
~		
+3	0 0 0 0 0 0 1 1	0 0 0 0 0 0 1 1
+2	0 0 0 0 0 0 1 0	0 0 0 0 0 0 1 0
+1	0 0 0 0 0 0 0 1	0 0 0 0 0 0 0 1
+0	0 0 0 0 0 0 0 0	0 0 0 0 0 0 0 0
-0	0 0 0 0 0 0 0 0	1 0 0 0 0 0 0 0
-1	1 1 1 1 1 1 1 1	1 0 0 0 0 0 0 1
-2	1 1 1 1 1 1 1 0	1 0 0 0 0 0 1 0
-3	1 1 1 1 1 1 0 1	1 0 0 0 0 0 1 1
~		
-127	1 0 0 0 0 0 0 1	1 1 1 1 1 1 1 1
-128	1 0 0 0 0 0 0 0	

Table 1. 2's complement and folded binary code for representing 8 bit speech data.

As shown in this table, an 8 bit speech data encoded in the 2's complement ranges from -128 to +127. On the other hand, an 8 bit speech data encoded in the folded binary code ranges from -127 to +127. Although the folded binary code cannot represent -128, it may represent both +0 and -0 instead. This redundancy can be a container for embedding secret message without any degradation.

The embedding procedure of the proposed technique is programmed in C language as shown in Fig. 2. In this procedure, b represents a 1 bit secret message and c represents an 8bit cover data encoded in the folded binary code. The proposed technique is categorized as a lossless steganography technique, since it does not degrade cover data by embedding secret message.

```
if ((c & 0x7F) == 0)
{
  if (b == 0) c &= 0x7F;
  if (b == 1) c |= 0x80;
}
```

Fig. 2. Embedding procedure of the proposed technique programmed in C language.

4. G.711

G.711 is the most common codec for telephony speech standardized by ITU-T (International Telecommunication Union Telecommunication Standardization Sector) (ITU-T, 1988). It consists of μ-law and A-law schemes designated as PCMU and PCMA, respectively. PCMU is mainly employed in North America and Japan. It encodes 14 bit speech data into 8 bit compression data at an 8 kHz sampling rate. PCMA is mainly employed in Europe. It encodes 13 bit speech data into 8 bit compression data at an 8 kHz sampling rate.

Figure 3 and 4 show the encoding and decoding procedure of PCMU. The compression data of PCMU consists of 1 bit sign, 3 bit exponent, and 4 bit mantissa (ITU-T, 2005). The compression data is encoded in the folded binary code. Table 2 shows some of the compression data and their corresponding speech data decoded with PCMU. As shown in this table, the speech data decoded with PCMU ranges from -0 to -8031, and +0 to +8031.

Figure 5 and 6 show the encoding and decoding procedure of PCMA. The compression data of PCMA consists of 1 bit sign, 3 bit exponent, and 4 bit mantissa (ITU-T, 2005). The compression data is encoded in the folded binary code. Table 2 shows some of the

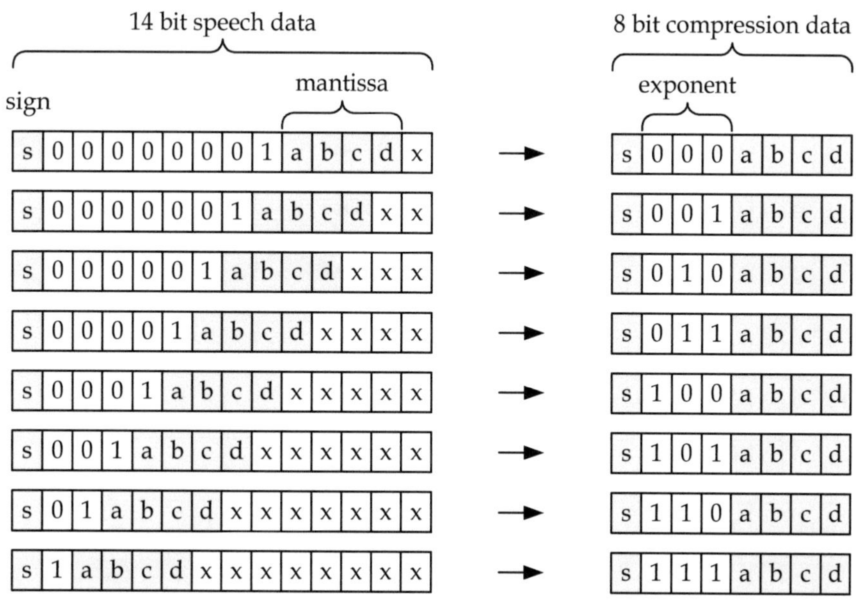

Fig. 3. Encoding procedure of PCMU.

compression data and their corresponding speech data decoded with PCMA. As shown in this table, the speech data decoded with PCMA ranges from -1 to -4032, and +1 to +4032.

Note that there is an overlap in the speech data decoded with PCMU. On the other hand, there is no such an overlap in the speech data decoded with PCMA. This indicates that a lossless steganography technique is available for PCMU, although it is not for PCMA.

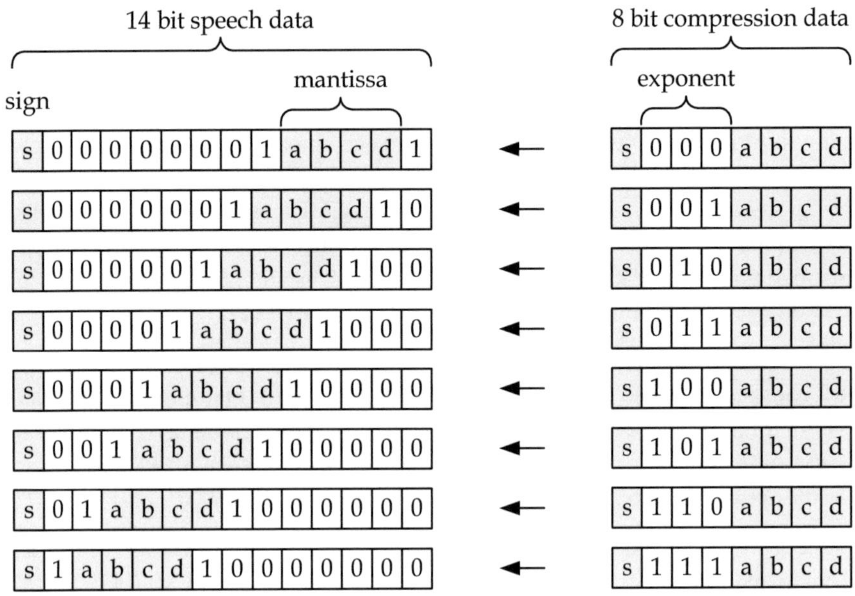

Fig. 4. Decoding procedure of PCMU.

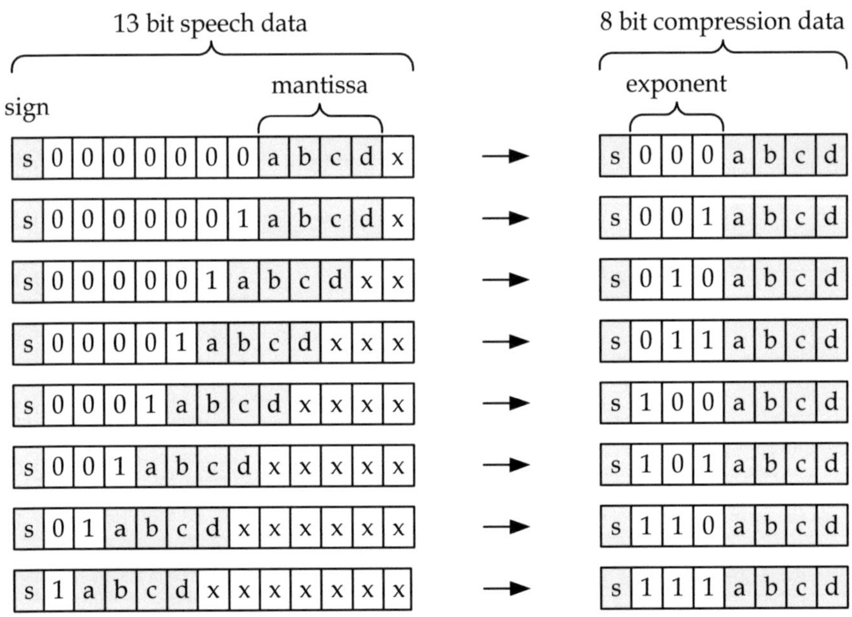

Fig. 5. Encoding procedure of PCMA.

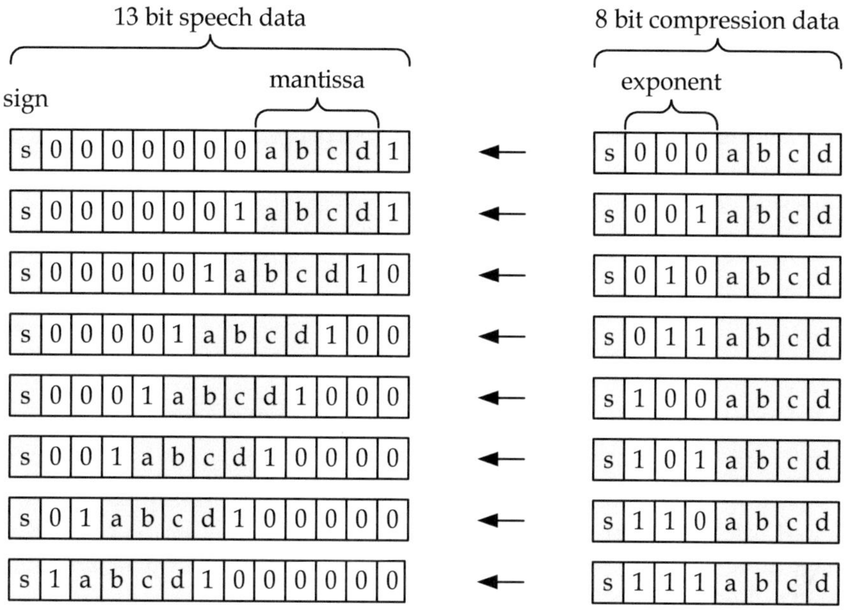

Fig. 6. Decoding procedure of PCMA.

compression data	decoded speech data (PCMU)	decoded speech data (PCMA)
+127	+8031	+4032
~		
+3	+6	+7
+2	+4	+5
+1	+2	+3
+0	+0	+1
-0	-0	-1
-1	-2	-3
-2	-4	-5
-3	-6	-7
~		
-127	-8031	-4032

Table 2. Speech data decoded with PCMU and PCMA.

5. Lossless steganography technique for G.711

Taking account of the characteristic of PCMU, secret message can be embedded into both +0 and -0 in the compression data without any degradation. When 0 is required to be embedded, the sign bit of the compression data is changed to be 0. This means that the compression data is changed to be +0. When 1 is required to be embedded, the sign bit of the compression data is changed to be 1. This means that the compression data is changed to be -0. The embedding procedure of the proposed technique is defined as follows.

$$c = \begin{cases} +0 & (|c| = 0, b = 0) \\ -0 & (|c| = 0, b = 1) \end{cases} \tag{1}$$

where b represents a 1 bit secret message and c represents an 8 bit compression data. This procedure is programmed in C language as shown in Fig. 7.

Figure 8 shows an example of the proposed technique. The compression data is represented as white and black circles according to the sign bit. The sign bit of the compression data represented by white circle is 0. On the other hand, the sign bit of the compression data represented by black circle is 1.

This example shows 4 candidates that can contain 4 bit secret message in total. According to their sign bits, these data originally contain 4 bit secret message represented as (0, 0, 1, 1). In order to embed secret message represented as (0, 1, 0, 1), the proposed technique changes these data as shown in Fig. 8. Since all of these are decoded to be 0 even if their sign bits are changed, the proposed technique does not degrade the speech quality at all.

```
if ((c & 0x7F) == 0)
{
  if (b == 0) c &= 0x7F;
  if (b == 1) c |= 0x80;
}
```

Fig. 7. Embedding procedure of the proposed technique programmed in C language.

6. DVI-ADPCM

The concept of the proposed technique may potentially be applicable to other codecs that also employ the folded binary code. Another example is DVI-ADPCM. Not only G.711 but also DVI-ADPCM is employed in telephony communications as a standard VoIP (Voice over IP) codec (RFC, 1996).

(a)

(b)

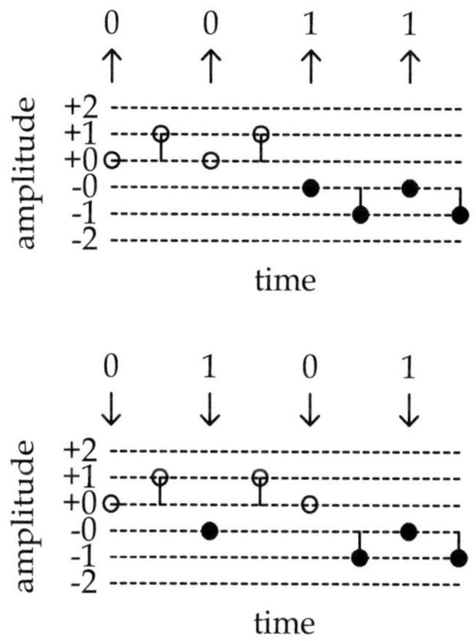

Fig. 8. Example of the proposed technique: (a) compression data before embedding, and (b) compression data after embedding.

DVI-ADPCM is a speech codec based on the ADPCM (Adaptive Differential Pulse Code Modulation) algorithm developed by DVI (Intel's Digital Video Interactive Group) (Microsoft, 1994). The block diagram of the ADPCM algorithm is shown in Fig. 9. In this diagram, $x(n)$ represents a speech data and $c(n)$ represents a compression data at the time of n.

DVI-ADPCM is designated as DVI3 and DVI4 according to the size of compression data. DVI3 encodes 16 bit speech data into 3 bit compression data at an 8 kHz sampling rate. DVI4 encodes 16 bit speech data into 4 bit compression data at an 8 kHz sampling rate. The compression data of DVI3 consists of 1 bit sign and 2 bit magnitude. The compression data of DVI4 consists of 1 bit sign and 3 bit magnitude. Both of these are encoded in the folded binary code.

Figure 10 and 11 show the decoding procedure of DVI3 and DVI4 programmed in C language. In these procedures, c is a compression data, x is a speech data, d is a difference between the previous and the current speech data, and s is a step size (Microsoft, 1994).

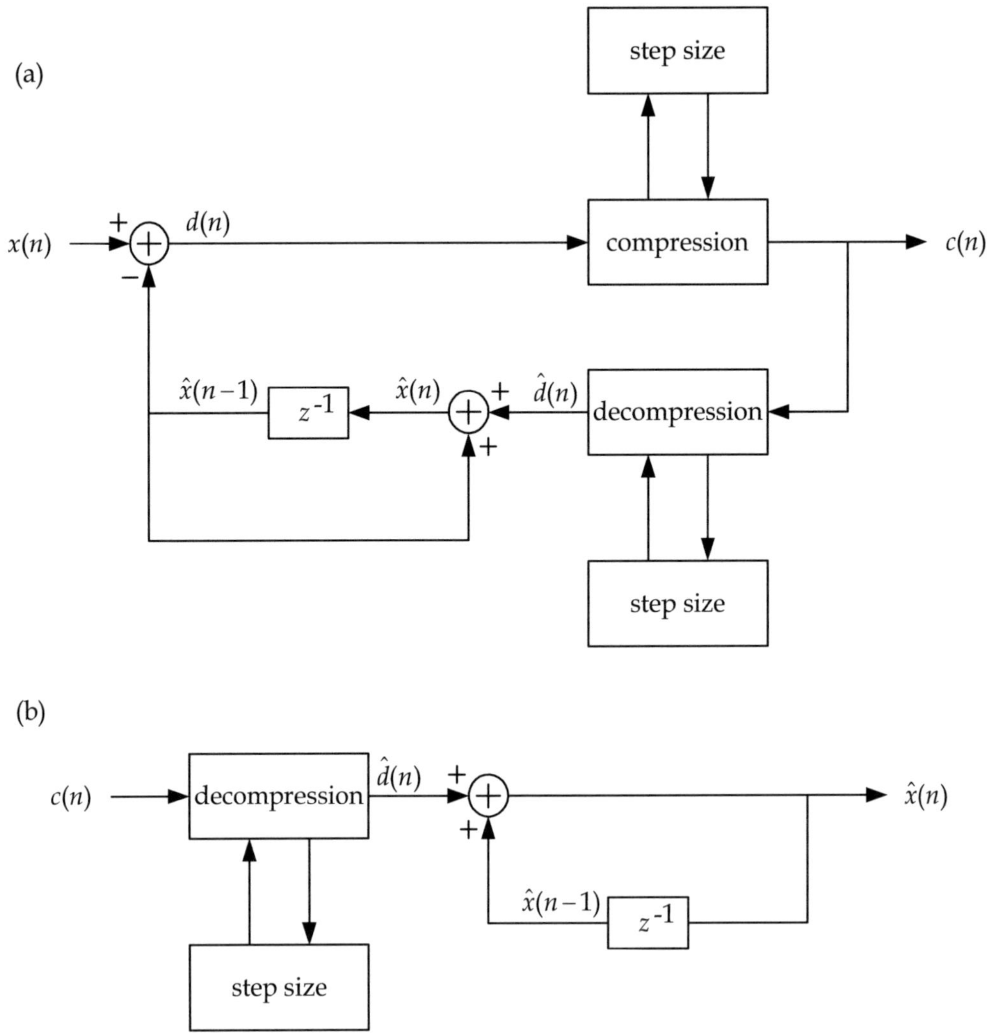

Fig. 9. Block diagram of ADPCM: (a) encoding procedure, and (b) decoding procedure.

```
d = s >> 2;
if (c & 0x1) d += s >> 1;
if (c & 0x2) d += s;
if (c & 0x4) d = -d;
x += d;
```

Fig. 10. Decoding Procedure of DVI3 programmed in C language.

```
d = s >> 3;
if (c & 0x1) d += s >> 2;
if (c & 0x2) d += s >> 1;
if (c & 0x4) d += s;
if (c & 0x8) d = -d;
x += d;
```

Fig. 11. Decoding Procedure of DVI4 programmed in C language.

7. Lossless steganography technique for DVI-ADPCM

The step size of DVI-ADPCM ranges from 7 to 32767 as shown in Fig.12 (Microsoft, 1994). When the magnitude of the compression data is 0 and the step size is 7, the speech data decoded with DVI4 does not depend on the sign of the compression data. This condition allows a lossless steganography technique that can embed secret message without any degradation. The embedding procedure of the proposed technique is defined as follows.

```
int s[89] =
{
  7, 8, 9, 10, 11, 12, 13, 14,
  16, 17, 19, 21, 23, 25, 28, 31,
  34, 37, 41, 45, 50, 55, 60, 66,
  73, 80, 88, 97, 107, 118, 130, 143,
  157, 173, 190, 209, 230, 253, 279, 307,
  337, 371, 408, 449, 494, 544, 598, 658,
  724, 796, 876, 963, 1060, 1166, 1282, 1411,
  1552, 1707, 1878, 2066, 2272, 2499, 2749, 3024,
  3327, 3660, 4026, 4428, 4871, 5358, 5894, 6484,
  7132, 7845, 8630, 9493, 10442, 11487, 12635, 13899,
  15289, 16818, 18500, 20350, 22385, 24623, 27086, 29794,
  32767
};
```

Fig. 12. Step size of DVI-ADPCM.

$$c = \begin{cases} +0 & (|c| = 0, s = 7, b = 0) \\ -0 & (|c| = 0, s = 7, b = 1) \end{cases} \tag{2}$$

where b represents a 1 bit secret message, c represents a 4 bit compression data, and s represents a step size. This procedure is programmed in C language as shown in Fig. 13.

Note that there is no such a condition that allows a lossless steganography technique for DVI3. This means that a lossless steganography technique is not available for DVI3 in the same manner of the proposed technique for DVI4.

```
if ((c & 0x7) == 0 && s == 7)
{
  if (b == 0) c &= 0x7;
  if (b == 1) c |= 0x8;
}
```

Fig. 13. Embedding procedure of the proposed technique programmed in C language.

8. Capacity of the proposed technique

The capacity of the proposed technique was evaluated by using speech data obtained from actual telephony environment, such as a private room, an office room, a cafeteria, and a railroad station. In these conditions, 8 male speech data (m1 – m8) and 8 female speech data (f1 – f8) were collected. As shown in Table 3, the duration of the speech data denoted as L was more than 120 s. The voice activity ratio of the speech data denoted as R was at around 50 %, since telephony speech generally shows the half duplex structure due to the alternate conversation process (Wright, 2001). RMS (Root Mean Square) of the background noise was calculated from voice inactive intervals.

	speech	L (s)	R (%)	RMS (dB)
private room	m1	134	51	-56.55
	m2	126	52	-59.66
	f1	124	57	-56.42
	f2	126	59	-55.72
office room	m3	127	48	-49.73
	m4	133	44	-48.59
	f3	123	49	-49.41
	f4	134	54	-48.04
cafeteria	m5	125	51	-37.48
	m6	136	48	-40.22
	f5	124	61	-37.37
	f6	123	67	-40.31
railroad station	m7	136	51	-33.87
	m8	129	68	-31.02
	f7	123	64	-34.03
	f8	126	54	-30.55

Table 3. Speech data obtained from actual telephony environment.

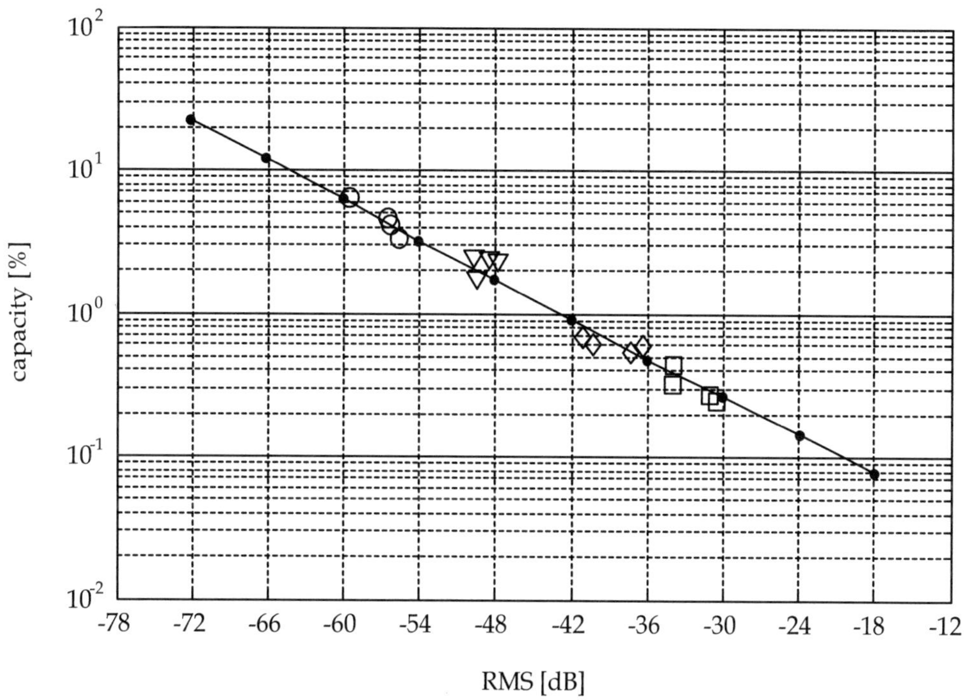

Fig. 14. Capacity of the proposed technique for PCMU: Circles, triangles, diamonds, and squares represent the capacity of a private room, an office room, a cafeteria, and a railroad station, respectively. Solid line represents the average capacity obtained from a simulation using a speech dialogue database.

The capacity of the proposed technique for PCMU is shown in Fig.14. This figure also shows a solid line that represents the average capacity obtained from a simulation using a speech dialogue database (ATR, 1997). It is indicated that the capacity of the proposed technique depends on the background noise in each telephony environment. The capacity ranges from 3.3 % to 6.4 % for the speech data obtained from a private room in which the background noise is almost imperceptible. It is interpreted that the capacity ranges from 264 bps to 512 bps in this condition. On the other hand, the capacity ranges from 0.24 % to 0.44 % for the speech data obtained from a railroad station in which the background noise is very annoying. It is interpreted that the capacity ranges from 19.2 bps to 35.2 bps in this condition.

The capacity of the proposed technique for DVI4 as well as PCMU is shown in Table 4. Compared with PCMU, the capacity for DVI4 is much smaller. Note that the capacity for DVI4 is very small even if the background noise is almost imperceptible. The capacity ranges from 0.029 % to 0.16 % for the speech data obtained from a private room. It is interpreted that the capacity ranges from 2.32 bps to 12.8 bps in this condition. On the other hand, there is no capacity for the speech data obtained from a cafeteria and a railroad station.

	speech	PCMU (%)	DVI4 (%)
private room	m1	4.7	0.058
	m2	6.4	0.16
	f1	4.3	0.038
	f2	3.3	0.029
office room	m3	2.5	0.0032
	m4	2.4	0.0013
	f3	1.7	0.0017
	f4	2.4	0.0012
cafeteria	m5	0.58	0
	m6	0.67	0
	f5	0.54	0
	f6	0.61	0
railroad station	m7	0.44	0
	m8	0.27	0
	f7	0.32	0
	f8	0.24	0

Table 4. Capacity of the proposed technique for PCMU and DVI4.

9. Semi-lossless steganography

Semi-lossless steganography technique is an idea for increasing the capacity of the proposed technique (Aoki, 2010b). This article describes how the capacity of the lossless steganography technique for PCMU can be increased by the semi-lossless steganography technique.

Figure 15 shows how the semi-lossless steganography technique embeds secret message. In the embedding procedure, this technique modifies an 8 bit compression data as follows.

$$c' = \begin{cases} c + j & (+0 \le c \le +127 - j) \\ c - j & (-127 + j \le c \le -0) \end{cases} \tag{3}$$

where j (≥0) represents the amplitude modification level.

The amplitude modification may cause undesirable clipping in the 8 bit compression data, if its magnitude exceeds 127-j. Consequently, this technique can recover the original speech data only when the amplitude of the 8 bit compression data ranges from -127+j to +127-j.

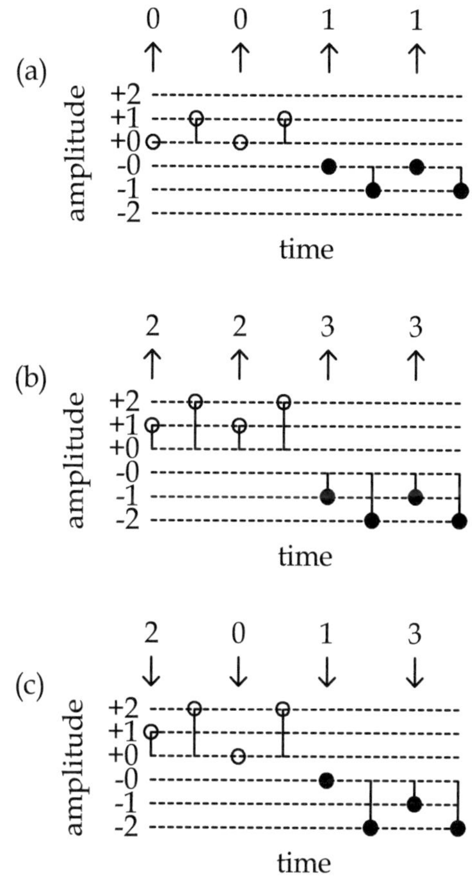

Fig. 15. Embedding procedure of the semi-lossless steganography technique:
(a) compression data before embedding, (b) amplitude modification, and (c) compression data after embedding.

Most of the practical cases meet this condition when the amplitude modification level is small enough. This is based on the fact that the amplitude of speech data statistically shows the exponential distribution (Rabiner, 1978). In general, the maximum magnitude of the 8 bit compression data is less than 127-j.

In this sense, this technique can be categorized as a reversible steganography technique, if this condition is satisfied. However, if this condition is not satisfied, this technique cannot recover the original speech data any more. Therefore, this technique is named semi-lossless steganography technique in this study.

The embedding procedure of the semi-lossless steganography technique is defined as follows.

$$c' = \begin{cases} +j & (|c'| = j, b = 2^j) \\ \vdots & \\ +1 & (|c'| = j, b = 2) \\ +0 & (|c'| = j, b = 0) \\ -0 & (|c'| = j, b = 1) \\ -1 & (|c'| = j, b = 3) \\ \vdots & \\ -j & (|c'| = j, b = 2^j + 1) \end{cases} \tag{4}$$

The capacity of the lossless steganography technique is defined as N bit, where N represents the number of the compression data in which the secret message can be embedded. On the other hand, the capacity of the semi-lossless steganography technique is defined as $N(\log_2(j+1)+1)$ bit. The capacity of the semi-lossless steganography technique increases according to the amplitude modification level. However, undesirable clipping may occur more frequently in such a situation.

After the extracting procedure of the secret message, the semi-lossless steganography technique recovers the 8 bit compression data as follows.

$$c = \begin{cases} c' - j & (+j < c' \leq +127) \\ 0 & (-j \leq c' \leq +j) \\ c' + j & (-127 \leq c' < -j) \end{cases} \tag{5}$$

Of course, the recovery procedure is necessary for decoding the original speech data. However, this procedure is omitted in the conventional telephony systems that do not implement the semi-lossless steganography technique. In such a situation, there is no way to remove the degradation from the speech data.

In order to evaluate such degradation, this study investigated the quality of the modified speech data by using PESQ (Perceptual Evaluation of Speech Quality) (ITU-T, 2001). PESQ is widely employed as an objective evaluation measure of the speech quality in telephony communications. Taking account of the characteristics of human auditory perception, PESQ positively correlates with a subjective evaluation measure such as MOS (Mean Opinion Score). PESQ score ranges from 4.5 to -0.5. The higher the PESQ score, the better the speech quality.

Figure 16 shows the average PESQ scores with 95 % confidence intervals. These were calculated from the 16 speech data employed in the evaluation for the capacity of the proposed technique.

As shown in this figure, it is indicated that the amplitude modification causes some degradation. However, it is almost imperceptible when the amplitude modification level is small enough. This result may potentially assure the compatibility of the semi-lossless steganography technique with the conventional telephony systems. This means that normal playback of the speech data modified with the proposed technique is still acceptable in the conventional telephony systems that do not implement the semi-lossless steganography technique.

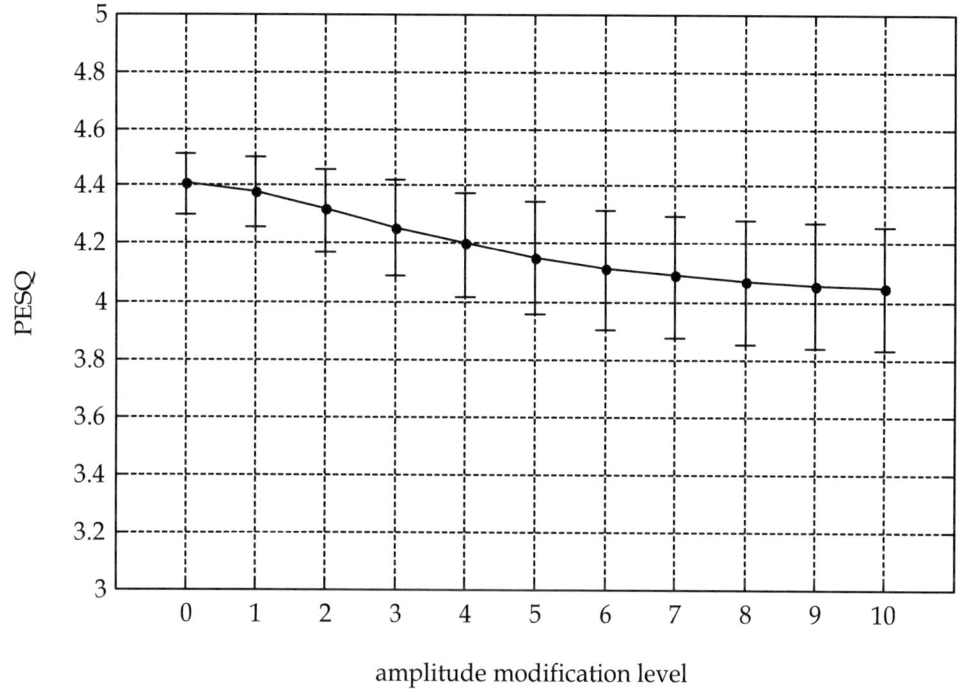

Fig. 16. Degradation of speech data by amplitude modification.

10. Conclusion

This article described an idea for the lossless steganography technique based on the characteristic of the folded binary code employed in several speech codecs, such as G.711 and DVI-ADPCM. In addition, an idea for the semi-lossless steganography technique is also described.

The proposed techniques take advantage of the redundancy of the speech codecs. It is a sort of the loophole of the speech codecs that can be employed as a container of secret message. Such a loophole plays an important role for embedding secret message without any degradation.

The concept of the proposed technique may potentially be applicable to other codecs that also employ the folded binary code. Besides G.711 and DVI-ADPCM, it is of interest to find out the codecs in which the proposed technique is available. In addition, it is also of interest to develop some practical applications that employ the proposed technique for transmitting secret message. Both of these topics are the future works of this study.

11. Acknowledgment

The author would like to express the gratitude to the Ministry of Education, Culture, Sports, Science and Technology of Japan for providing a grant (no.21760270) toward this study.

12. References

Aoki, N. (2003). A packet loss concealment technique for VoIP using steganography based on pitch waveform replication, IEICE Transactions on Communications, vol.J86-B, no.12, pp. 2551-2560

Aoki, N. (2006). A band extension technique for G.711 speech using steganography, IEICE Transactions on Communications, vol.E89-B, no.6, pp. 1896-1898

Aoki, N. (2007). A band extension technique for G.711 speech using steganography based on full wave rectification, IEICE Transactions on Communications, vol.J90-B, no.7, pp.697-704

Aoki, N. (2007). A technique of lossless steganography for G.711, IEICE Transactions on Communications, vol.E90-B, no.11, pp. 3271-3273

Aoki, N. (2008). A technique of lossless steganography for G.711 telephony speech, 2008 Fourth International Conference on Intelligent Information Hiding and Multimedia Signal Processing (IIHMSP2008), Harbin, China, pp.608-611

Aoki, N. (2009). Lossless steganography techniques for IP telephony speech taking account of the redundancy of folded binary code, AICIT 2009 Fifth International Joint Conference on INC, IMS and IDC (NCM2009), Seoul, Korea, pp.1689-1692

Aoki, N. (2009). A lossless steganography technique for G.711 telephony speech, 2009 APSIPA Annual Summit and Conference (APSIPA ASC 2009), Sapporo, Japan, pp. 274-277

Aoki, N. (2010). A lossless steganography technique for DVI-ADPCM Transactions on Fundamentals of Electronics, Communications and Computer Sciences, vol.J93-A, no.2, pp. 104-106

Aoki, N. (2010). A semi-lossless steganography technique for G.711 telephony speech, 2010 Sixth International Conference on Intelligent Information Hiding and Multimedia Signal Processing (IIHMSP2010), Darmstadt, Germany, pp. 534-537

Aoki, N. (2012). Enhancement of speech quality in telephony communications by steganography, Multimedia Information Hiding Technologies and Methodologies for Controlling Data, IGI Global (To be published)

ATR (1997). Speech Dialogue Database for Spontaneous Speech Recognition

Cox, I., Miller, M., Bloom, J., Fridrich, J., and Kalker, T. (2008). Digital Watermarking and Steganography, Second Edition, Morgan Kaufmann Publishers

ITU-T (1988). G.711, Pulse code modulation (PCM) of voice frequencies

ITU-T (2001). P.862, Perceptual evaluation of speech quality (PESQ), an objective method for end-to-end speech quality assessment of narrow-band telephone networks and speech codecs

ITU-T (2005). G.191, Software tools for speech and audio coding standardization

Microsoft (1994). Multimedia Data Standards Update

Rabiner, L.R. and Schafer, R.W. (1978). Digital Processing of Speech Signals, Prentice-Hall.

RFC (1996). RFC1890, RTP profile for audio and video conferences with minimal control

Wright, D.J. (2001). Voice over Packet Networks, John Wiley & Sons